Joel G. Siegel, Ph.D.,
CPA, Professor of Finance
Queens College
and Jae K. Shim, Ph.D.,
Professor of Finance
California State University,
Long Beach

Finance

D1304908

BARRON'S

New York • London • Toronto • Sydney

All inquiries should be addressed to:
Barron's Educational Series, Inc.
250 Wireless Boulevard
Hauppauge, New York 11788

Library of Congress Catalog Card No. 90-27725

International Standard Book No. 0-8120-4596-3

Library of Congress Cataloging in Publication Data
Siegel, Joel G.
    Study keys to finance / by Joel G. Siegel and Jae K. Shim.
        p.   cm.—(Barron's study keys)
    Includes index.
    ISBN 0-8120-4596-3
    1. Finance. I. Shim, Jae K. II. Title. III. Series.
HG173.S515   1991
332'.076—dc20   90-27725
                                                                    CIP

PRINTED IN THE UNITED STATES OF AMERICA
1234   5500   987654321

CONTENTS

Theme 1 INTRODUCTION

*F*inance involves obtaining, using, and managing funds to achieve the entity's financial objectives. Funds may be obtained from money markets and capital markets. The various types of business organizations include sole proprietorship, partnership, and corporations. Tax planning is important to minimize taxes. The company must take advantage of all allowable tax deductions, including depreciation, write-offs for promotion and entertainment, and contributions.

INDIVIDUAL KEYS IN THIS THEME	
1	Introduction to finance
2	Basic forms of business organizations
3	Financial institutions and markets
4	Depreciation methods
5	Federal corporate taxation

Key 1   Introduction to finance

OVERVIEW   *Finance covers financial analysis and planning, investment decisions, financing and capital structure decisions, and management of financial resources.*

Goals of managerial finance: 1. stockholder wealth maximization, 2. profit maximization, 3. managerial reward maximization, 4. behavioral goals, and 5. social responsibility.

Modern managerial finance theory: assumes that the primary goal of the firm is to maximize the wealth of its stockholders, i.e., to maximize the price of the firm's common stock.

Profit maximization: a short-term goal. A firm may maximize its short-term profits at the expense of its long-term profitability.

Stockholder wealth maximization: a long-term goal. Wealth maximization is generally preferred because it considers 1. wealth for the long term, 2. risk or uncertainty, 3. the timing of returns, and 4. the stockholders' return.

Financial manager's responsibilities:
- Determining the proper amount of funds to employ in the firm, i.e., the size of the firm and its rate of growth
- Allocating funds efficiently to specific assets
- Raising funds on as favorable terms as possible, i.e., determining the composition of liabilities
- Managing working capital, like inventory and accounts receivable

Treasurer: handles external financing matters and is responsible for managing corporate assets and liabilities, planning the finances, budgeting capital, financing the business, formulating credit policy, and managing the investment portfolio.

Controller: concerned with internal matters—financial and cost accounting, taxes, budgeting, and control functions.

Financial vice president: supervises all phases of financial activity and serves as financial adviser to the board of directors.

Effects: Financial managers influence:
- Present and future earnings per share (EPS)
- The timing, duration, and risk of these earnings
- Dividend policy
- The manner of financing the firm

Key 2 Basic forms of business organizations

OVERVIEW *The basic forms of business organizations are: sole proprietorship, partnership, and corporation.*

Sole proprietorship: a business owned by one individual.
- *Advantages:* 1. requires no formal charter, 2. has minimal organizational costs, and 3. profits and control not shared with others.
- *Disadvantages*: 1. limited ability to raise large sums of money, 2. unlimited liability, and 3. limited life.

Partnership: similar to sole proprietorship but more than one owner.
- *Advantages:* 1. minimal organization effort and costs, and 2. few government regulations.
- *Disadvantages:* 1. unlimited liability, 2. limited ability to raise large sums of money, and 3. dissolved upon the death or withdrawal of any of the partners.

Limited partnership: one or more partners, some with limited liability up to their investment if business fails. *Example:* real estate.
- General partner manages the business.
- Limited partners not involved in daily activities.
- Limited partners receive return in the form of income and capital gains.
- Often receives tax benefits.

Corporation: a legal entity existing apart from its owners (stockholders). Ownership evidenced by possession of shares of stock.
- *Advantages:* 1. unlimited life, 2. limited liability, 3. transfer of ownership through stock transfer, and 4. ability to raise large sums of capital.
- *Disadvantages:* 1. difficult and costly to establish, and 2. subject to double taxation on earnings and dividends paid to stockholders.

Subchapter S corporation: a form of corporation whose stockholders are taxed as partners. Distributes its income directly to shareholders; avoids corporate income tax while enjoying the other advantages of the corporate form. To qualify as an S corporation, a corporation must:
- Have fewer than 35 shareholders; none may be nonresident foreigners
- Have only one class of stock
- Properly elect Subchapter S status

Key 3 Financial institutions and markets

OVERVIEW *A healthy economy depends on efficient transfer of funds from savers to individuals, businesses, and governments. Most transfers occur through specialized financial institutions that serve as intermediaries between suppliers and users of funds.*

Financial markets: provide a mechanism through which the financial manager may obtain funds from a wide range of sources, including financial institutions.
- Entities demanding funds are brought together with those having surplus funds.
- The financial markets are composed of *money markets* and *capital markets*.

Money markets: credit markets for short-term (less than 1 year) debt securities, usually highly liquid securities with relatively low default risk. Equity instruments such as common stock are not traded here. *Examples:* U.S. Treasury bills, federal agency securities, bankers' acceptances, and commercial paper.

Capital markets: markets in which long-term debt and equity securities issued by the government and corporations are traded. Capital market instruments often carry greater default and market risks but return a higher yield than money market instruments. *Examples:* New York Stock Exchange and regional stock exchanges.
- Over-the-counter (or unlisted) market is an informal system of contacts among brokers and dealers.
- Most corporate bonds are traded over the counter.

Primary market: market for new issues.

Secondary market: market for previously issued, "secondhand" securities. *Example:* New York Stock Exchange.

Other financial markets:
- Market for special types of financial instruments
- Commodity market: handles various commodities futures
- Foreign exchange market: handles international financial transactions between the U.S. and other countries
- Mortgage market: handles real estate financing and mortgage-backed securities

Key 4 Depreciation methods

OVERVIEW *Depreciation spreads the original cost of a fixed asset over its estimated life. Examples of fixed assets are plant, equipment, and vehicles. Depreciation reduces taxable income. Accelerated depreciation methods provide more rapid expensing of the cost of the asset and thereby offer the advantage of deferring the payment of taxes.*

Straight-line method: results in equal periodic depreciation charges. Most appropriate when an asset's usage is uniform from period to period, as is the case with furniture.

$$\text{Depreciation expense} = \frac{\text{Cost} - \text{salvage value}}{\text{Number of years of useful life}}$$

Sum-of-the years' digits method (SYD): the number of years of life expectancy enumerated in reverse order in the numerator; the denominator is the sum of the digits. *Example:* If the life expectancy of a machine is 5 years, list the numbers of years in reverse order (5,4,3,2,1) and total them. The sum of these digits is 15. Thus, the fraction for the first year is $\frac{5}{15}$, while the fraction for the last year is $\frac{1}{15}$. The sum of the five fractions equals $\frac{15}{15}$, or 1. At the end of 5 years, the machine is completely written down to its salvage value.

KEY FORMULA

To find the sum-of-the-years' digits (S):

$$S = \frac{(N)\,(N+1)}{2},\text{ where N is the number of years of expected life}$$

Double-declining-balance method (DDB): Depreciation expense is highest in the earlier years and lowest in the later years. The computation follows:
- A depreciation rate is determined by doubling the straight-line rate. *Example:* The double-declining rate for a 10-year asset is 20% (10% × 2).
- Depreciation equals the rate multiplied by the book value of the asset at the beginning of the period.
- The method ignores salvage value in the computation.

Key 5 Federal corporate taxation

OVERVIEW *Taxes affect financing and investment decisions. Tax planning minimizes tax obligations and postpones the payment of taxes. Corporations file federal tax returns on IRS Form 1120.*

Tax strategies and planning: Analyze the tax consequences of alternative approaches in decision making. Shift income and expenses into tax years that will result in the least tax.
- Receive income in a year in which it will be taxed at a lower rate.
- Pay tax-deductible expenses in a year in which tax rates are high.
- Accelerate expenses that are deductible or that will be restricted in the future.
- Try to invest income in tax-free instruments. *Example:* Interest on a municipal bond is partially or totally tax-free.

Taxable income: gross income from revenue sources less tax-deductible expenses.

Tax rates: the rates applied to taxable income to determine tax.
- *Marginal tax rate:* tax rate on the next dollar of income.
- *Effective tax rate:* average tax rate on all taxable income equal to the tax divided by the taxable income.

Income subject to tax: 1. capital gains (or losses) on the sale of a capital asset (e.g., stock), 2. sales, 3. professional fees earned, 4. interest income, 5. dividend income, and 6. lease, rental, and maintenance income.

Tax deductions: 1. business meal and entertainment expenses (80% deductible), 2. food and entertainment-related employee benefits, 3. promotional items, 4. business gifts (up to $25 per recipient), 5. charitable contributions up to 10% of taxable income, 6. insurance payments, 7. depreciation, 8. interest, 9. professional fees, 10. pension expense, 11. casualty and theft losses, and 12. actual bad debts.

Foreign tax credit: credit for taxes paid to a foreign government.

Theme 2. FINANCIAL STATEMENTS AND ANALYSIS

A company is required to include in its annual report a balance sheet, income statement, and statement of cash flows. These financial statements enable readers to know the financial health of the business and its operating performance for the period. The balance sheet reveals what a company owns and owes, while the income statement reports revenues and expenses. The statement of cash flows divides the sources and uses of cash into operating, investing, and financing activities. Financial statement analysis involves looking at a company's liquidity, asset utilization, solvency, profitability, and dividend history.

Key 6 Basic financial statements

OVERVIEW *Financial statements depict a company's financial position and operating performance so that management, investors, and creditors can appraise the financial health of the business. The two major financial statements are the income statement and balance sheet. These financial statements help reveal the company's profit, what it owns, what it owes, and the stockholders' equity.*

Income statement: reports net income, or profit, earned (total revenue minus total expenses).
- *Revenue:* increase in capital from sale of merchandise (sales), performance of services (e.g., professional fees earned), or passive income (e.g., interest income, dividend income).
- *Expense:* decrease in capital from activities necessary to generate revenue. *Examples:* 1. cost of the inventory sold (cost of sales), 2. value of the services rendered (e.g., salary expense, fringe benefits), 3. expenditure necessary for conducting business operations (e.g., rent expense, telephone expense), 4. financial expenses (e.g., interest expense), and 5. taxes.

Balance sheet: lists assets, liabilities, and stockholders' equity.
- *Assets:* what a company owns, including: 1. *current assets* (assets expected to be converted into cash or used up within one year, such as inventory), 2. *long-term investments* (investments in other companies' stocks or bonds where the intent is to hold them for more than one year), 3. *property, plant and equipment* (tangible assets having physical substance employed in the production of goods or services and having a life greater than one year, such as machinery), and 4. *intangible assets* (assets with a life exceeding one year that either lack physical substance or arise from a right granted by the government, such as a patent).
- *Liabilities:* what the company owes, including *current liabilities* (liabilities due within one year such as accounts payable) and *noncurrent liabilities* (liabilities due within a period greater than one year, such as bonds payable).
- *Stockholders' equity:* equity of the stockholders in the business. (See Key 7.)

Key 7 Stockholders' equity section of the balance sheet

OVERVIEW *The stockholders' equity section shows the ownership interest of stockholders in the corporation—the extent to which company assets are financed by equity issues rather than debt issues. Stockholders' equity is the difference between total assets and total liabilities.*

Stockholders' equity section: shows transactions affecting stockholders and includes:
- Capital Stock
- Plus: Paid-in-Capital
- Plus: Retained Earnings
- Plus or Minus: Foreign Currency Translation Gain or Loss
- Minus: Unrealized Loss on Long-term Investment Portfolio
- Total
- Minus: Treasury Stock
- Equals: Total Stockholders' Equity

Components of stockholders' equity:
- *Capital stock:* stock issued by the corporation and stated at par value, as well as stock to be issued at a later date. *Examples:* preferred stock, common stock, stock options, stock warrants, and stock dividends.
- *Paid-in-capital:* the excess over par value received for the issuance of stock.
- *Retained earnings:* the accumulated earnings of the company less any dividends paid out.
- *Foreign currency translation gain or loss:* gain or loss from translating foreign financial statements in the foreign currency to U.S. dollars.
- *Unrealized loss on long-term investment portfolio:* unrealized (holding) decline in value from cost to market value of the investment portfolio.
- *Treasury stock:* issued shares that have been reacquired.

Key 8 Statement of cash flows

OVERVIEW *Financial analysis involves 1. financial ratio analysis, using the balance sheet and income statement, and 2. analysis of cash flows, using the statement of cash flows. This statement classifies cash receipts and cash payments as arising from operating, investing, and financing activities.*

Some questions answered by the statement of cash flows:
- Where did the earnings go?
- Why was money borrowed?
- Why were the cash dividends not larger?
- How was the expansion in productive capacity financed?
- How was debt retired?
- What became of the proceeds of a bond or equity issue?

Definition of cash: cash and cash equivalents. A cash equivalent is a short-term liquid investment having an original maturity of 3 months or less. *Examples:* Treasury bills and commercial paper.

Operating section: Operating activities relate to manufacturing and selling goods or rendering services.
- Cash flow derived from operating activities typically applies to the cash effects of transactions entering into profit determination.
- Cash inflows from operating activities include: 1. cash sales or collections on accounts receivable, and 2. cash received from interest income and dividend income.
- Cash outflows from operating activities include: 1. cash paid for inventory or on accounts payable, and 2. cash paid for operating expenses.

Investing section: cash flows applicable to changes in long-term assets. Investing activities include purchasing or selling debt and equity securities in other entities and buying and selling fixed assets.

Financing section: cash flows resulting from changes in long-term liabilities and stockholders' equity items. Financing activities include:
- Issuance or repurchase of the company's own stock
- Issuance or retirement of long-term debt
- Payment of dividends

Key 9 Horizontal and vertical analysis

OVERVIEW *Horizontal and vertical analysis are part of financial statement analysis. Horizontal analysis looks at trends in the accounts over the years. Vertical analysis uses a significant item on a financial statement as a base value and compares all other items on the common size financial statement to it.*

Horizontal analysis: the percentage change in an account computed to reveal trends. Percentage change equals the dollar change over the prior year amount. *Example:* Sales in 19X1 and 19X2 were $100,000 and $120,000, respectively. The percentage change is 20% ($20,000/$100,000).
- It identifies areas of wide divergence to be investigated.
- The dollar amount of the change and the percentage change are both important to look at because either one alone might be misleading.
- When an analysis covers many years of comparative financial statements, it may be best to show trends relative to a base year. The base year is the one most representative of the company's activity. *Example:* 19X3 is the base year and total assets are $400,000. If total assets in 19X8 are $500,000, the index in 19X8 is 1.25 ($500,000/$400,000).
- It compares trends in the company's accounts to those of competitors and to industry norms.

Vertical analysis: compares a financial statement item to a base amount within the same year.
- In the balance sheet, total assets are assigned 100%; each asset is expressed as a percentage of total assets. Similarly, each liability and stockholders' equity account is expressed as a percentage of total liabilities and stockholders' equity respectively.
- In the income statement, net sales is assigned 100%; all other income statement accounts are evaluated in comparison to it.

Key 10 Liquidity and liquidity ratios

OVERVIEW *Liquidity is the firm's ability to convert noncash assets into cash or to obtain cash to meet impending obligations.*

Seasonal: For seasonal businesses, year-end financial data may not be representative; averages based on quarterly information may be used to level out seasonal effects.

Net working capital: current assets less current liabilities. Working capital is a safety cushion for creditors and a reserve for unexpected contingencies.

Current ratio: current assets divided by current liabilities. It reveals the company's ability to meet current liabilities out of current assets.

Quick ratio: A stringent test of liquidity that looks at the most liquid current assets, excluding inventory and prepaid expenses; also called acid-test ratio. It equals:

$$\frac{\text{Cash} + \text{marketable securities} + \text{accounts receivable}}{\text{Current liabilities}}$$

Importance: Analyzing liquidity is essential for short-term creditors to ensure that the company has adequate funds to meet current debt. A company with poor liquidity is a credit risk.
- Liquidity is crucial to conducting business activity, especially in difficult times, such as when a business is shut down by a strike.
- Inadequate liquidity may lead to serious financial difficulties, including the inability to obtain financing or to meet obligations, such as operating expenses, that come due.

Key 11 Activity ratios

OVERVIEW   *Activity (asset utilization, turnover) ratios determine how fast asset accounts are converted into sales or cash. A greater utilization of assets results in higher profitability and cash flow and a lower risk of uncollectibility or obsolescence.*

Accounts receivable ratios and analysis:
* Accounts receivable turnover: number of times accounts receivable are collected during the year, equal to credit sales divided by average accounts receivable (the beginning balance plus the ending balance divided by two).
* A higher turnover indicates faster collection from customers.
* *Average accounts receivable collection period:* number of days it takes to collect on receivables, equal to 365 days divided by accounts receivable turnover.
* *Aging of accounts receivable:* lists accounts receivable according to the length of time they are outstanding. A longer period means more risk.

Inventory ratios and analysis:
* *Inventory Turnover:* number of times inventory is sold during the year, equal to cost of goods sold divided by average inventory.
* Lower turnover may result in buildup of merchandise and possible obsolescence.
* *Average age of inventory:* number of days inventory is held before sale, equal to 365 days divided by the inventory turnover.
* If age increases, 1. funds are tied up in inventory that could be invested elsewhere for a return, and 2. the company incurs higher carrying costs.

Operating cycle: number of days needed to convert inventory and accounts receivable to cash.

Fixed asset turnover: number of times fixed assets turn over into sales, equal to sales divided by average fixed assets.

Total asset turnover: number of times total assets turn over into sales, equal to sales divided by average total assets.

Key 12   Solvency and debt service
ratios

OVERVIEW   *Solvency (leverage, coverage) ratios reveal the company's ability to meet long-term obligations as they become due. Debt service ratios measure the firm's ability to cover finance charges created by its use of financial leverage. An analysis of solvency emphasizes the long-term financial and operating structure of the business. Solvency also depends upon corporate profitability.*

Debt level: When debt is excessive, the company may have problems meeting the interest payments and principal at maturity. If debt is too high, the maturity dates may be extended.
- The company enjoys a favorable leverage situation when the return on borrowed funds exceeds the after-tax interest cost, provided the debt level is reasonable.

Debt ratio: compares total liabilities to total assets. It shows the percentage of total funds obtained from creditors.

Debt/equity ratio: a measure of financial leverage and risk, equal to total liabilities divided by total stockholders' equity.

Noncurrent assets to noncurrent liabilities: A high ratio indicates protection for long-term creditors, because long-term debt will ultimately be paid out of long-term assets.

Times interest earned ratio: reflects the number of times before-tax earnings cover interest expense:

$$\frac{\text{Earnings before interest and taxes (EBIT)}}{\text{Interest expense}}$$

- Indicates how much of a decline in profits a company can absorb. *Example:* A ratio of 3 to 1 means that there is $3 in earnings available to cover $1 in interest.

Cash flow overall coverage ratio: A high ratio is desirable because it means the company has sufficient cash flow to meet its financial charges:

$$\frac{\text{EBIT} + \text{lease expense} + \text{depreciation}}{\text{Total financial charges}}$$

Key 13 Profitability ratios

OVERVIEW *Profitability ratios reveal the company's ability to earn a satisfactory profit and return on investment. The ratios are an indication of good financial health and how effectively the company is managing its assets.*

Gross profit margin: reveals the percentage of each dollar left over after the cost of sales:

$$\frac{\text{Gross profit}}{\text{Net sales}}$$

- Gross profit = Net sales − cost of sales

Profit margin: the ratio of net income to sales; a reflection of corporate earning power.
- The profit margin provides clues to a company's pricing, cost structure, and manufacturing efficiency.

Return on investment (ROI): Two ratios that evaluate ROI are:
- *Return on total assets (ROA):* indicates the efficiency with which management has used its resources to obtain income:

$$\frac{\text{Net income}}{\text{Average total assets}}$$

- *Return on Common Equity (ROE):* measures the rate of return earned on the common stockholders' investment:

$$\frac{\text{Net income} - \text{preferred dividends}}{\text{Average common stockholders' equity}}$$

Implications:
- Investors steer clear of companies with poor earnings potential because the poor earnings negatively impact market price of stock and dividends.
- Creditors avoid unprofitable companies because of a greater risk of default.
- Stockholders look at profitability as a key measure of operating performance.

Key 14 Du Pont system

OVERVIEW *The Du Pont system combines the income statement and balance sheet into either of two summary measures of performance: return on investment (ROI) and return on equity (ROE). There are two versions of the Du Pont System.*

The original Du Pont formula: The first version breaks down the return on investment (ROI) into net profit margin and total asset turnover:

$$\text{ROI} = \frac{\text{Net profit after taxes}}{\text{Total assets}} = \frac{\text{Net profit after taxes}}{\text{Sales}} \times \frac{\text{Sales}}{\text{Total assets}}$$

$$= \text{Net profit margin} \times \text{Total asset turnover}$$

The breakdown provides insights to financial managers on how to improve profitability and investment strategy.

Advantages of original Du Pont formula:
- Emphasizes the importance of turnover as a key to overall return on investment
- Recognizes the importance of sales
- Stresses the possibility of trading margin and turnover since they complement each other (weak margin can be complemented by a strong turnover, and vice versa)
- Indicates whether weaknesses are in profit margin, in turnover, or in both

Actions to improve ROI: 1. reduce expenses, 2. reduce assets, and 3. increase sales.
- Reducing expenses may mean improving productivity, automating, or cutting down on discretionary expenses.
- Reducing assets may mean better inventory control or speeding up collections.
- Increase sales while maintaining profit margin.

The modified Du Pont formula: The second version ties together the ROI and the degree of financial leverage as measured using the equity multiplier, the ratio of total assets to stockholders' equity, to determine the return on equity (ROE):

$$\text{ROE} = \frac{\text{Net profit after taxes}}{\text{Stockholders' equity}} = \frac{\text{Net profit after taxes}}{\text{Total assets}} \times \frac{\text{Total assets}}{\text{Stockholders' equity}}$$

$$= \quad \text{ROI} \quad \times \text{Equity multiplier}$$

Advantages of modified Du Pont formula:

- Enables the company to break its ROE into a profit-margin portion (net profit margin), an efficiency-of-asset-utilization portion (total asset turnover), and a use-of-leverage portion (equity multiplier).
- Helps determine what combination of asset return and leverage work best. Most companies try to keep a level roughly equal to what is considered normal within the industry.

Key 15   Market value ratios

OVERVIEW   *Market value ratios apply to a company's stock price relative to its earnings (or book value) per share, as well as to the dividend-related ratios.*

Earnings per share: amount of earnings for each common share held:

$$\frac{\text{Net income} - \text{preferred dividends}}{\text{Common shares outstanding}}$$

- An increase in EPS usually results in a rise in the market price of the stock and an increase in dividends.

Price-earnings ratio (multiple): market price per share divided by earnings per share.
- A high P/E ratio indicates investor confidence in the firm.
- A drop in the P/E ratio may result from several causes, including deteriorating financial health, increased risk, and industry problems.
- Some investors believe that if a company's P/E ratio is relatively low, the stock may be undervalued and represents a buying opportunity. Others believe that if the P/E ratio is relatively high, the stock may be overvalued and should be sold.

Book value per share: value of each share per the books based on historical cost:

$$\frac{\text{Total stockholders' equity} - \text{liquidation value of preferred stock}}{\text{Outstanding common shares}}$$

- If market price per share substantially exceeds book value per share, it may indicate good reception in the stock market.

Dividend ratios:
- *Dividend yield:* dividends per share divided by market price per share; shows return on a share of stock based on the current dividend rate and current price.
- *Dividend payout:* dividends per share divided by earnings per share; measures the portion of earnings paid out in dividends.
- A decline in the dividend ratios generally causes concern.

Key 16 Limitations of ratio analysis

OVERVIEW *The user of ratio analysis must take into account certain limitations when appraising a company's financial statements. Otherwise, the user may be misled by the ratios' implications.*

Limitations:
- Since financial statements are based on historical cost, they do not take into account inflation.
- Since ratios are static as of year-end, they do not consider future flows.
- A ratio does not reveal the quality of its components. *Example:* The current ratio may be high, but inventory may consist of obsolete goods.
- Diversity in accounting policies among companies can distort the ratios and make comparisons difficult. *Example:* Companies use different depreciation methods.
- The issuance of financial statements occurs several months after the end of the accounting year; figures may not reflect what is currently occurring in the business.
- A company may juggle figures to make the financial ratios look better. *Example:* A company may improve its current ratio shortly before year-end by paying a short-term debt.
- Financial statements do not take into account qualitative factors such as the quality of management, marketing aspects, economic conditions, and the political environment.
- Many large companies are engaged in multiple lines of business, making it difficult to identify the industry group the firm belongs. Comparing the ratios of such a company with those of other companies in one field may be meaningless.

Theme 3   BUDGETING AND FINANCIAL FORECASTING

A budget reveals management's expectations with regard to revenue and costs for a future period. It predicts the company's future cash position, taking into account anticipated cash inflows and cash outflows. Budgets are used for planning and control purposes. Companies prepare many types of budgets, including sales, production, costs, pro forma balance sheet, and pro forma income statement. Financial forecasts, the basis for budget preparation, start with sales and then predict costs, often as a percentage of those sales.

Key 17   Budgeting

OVERVIEW   *A comprehensive (master) budget is a formal statement of management's expectations regarding sales, expenses, volume, and other financial transactions. The cash budget helps management keep cash balances in reasonable relationships to its needs.*

Planning and control: At the beginning of the period, the budget is a plan or standard; at the end of the period, it serves as a control device to measure performance against the plan.

Types of budgets: The budget is either an *operating budget,* the result of operating decisions, or a *financial budget,* the result of financial decisions of the firm.
- The operating budget consists of: 1. sales budget, 2. production budget, 3. direct materials budget, 4. direct labor budget, 5. factory overhead budget, 6. selling and administrative expense budget, and 7. pro forma income statement.
- The financial budget consists of 1. cash budget, and 2. pro forma balance sheet.

Steps in the budgeting process:
1. Prepare a sales forecast.
2. Determine expected production volume.
3. Estimate manufacturing costs and operating expenses.
4. Determine cash flow and other financial effects.
5. Formulate projected financial statements.

The sales budget: starting point in preparing the master budget, since estimated sales volume influences nearly all other items in the master budget. The sales budget indicates the quantity of each product expected to be sold.
- The sales budget is constructed by multiplying expected sales in units by expected unit sales price.

The production budget: includes the number of units expected to be manufactured to meet budgeted sales and inventory requirements.
- The expected volume of production = the units expected to be sold + the desired inventory at the end of the period − the inventory at the beginning of the period.

The direct material budget: shows how much material will be required and how much must be purchased to meet production requirement.

The direct labor budget: Expected production volume for each period multiplied by the number of direct labor hours required to produce a single unit. The direct labor hours required to meet production requirements multiplied by the direct labor cost per hour yields budgeted total direct labor costs.

The factory overhead budget: schedule of all manufacturing costs other than direct materials and direct labor.

The selling and administrative expense budget: list of operating expenses in selling the products and in managing the business.

The budgeted income statement: summarizes the various component projections of revenue and expenses.

The budgeted balance sheet: shows expected assets, liabilities, and stockholders' equity.

Computer-based models for budgeting: help build a budget for profit planning and answer a variety of "what-if" scenarios, providing a basis for choice among alternatives under conditions of uncertainty.

The cash budget: helps avoid idle cash and possible cash shortages. To meet its main objective, sound projections of cash collections from customers and cash expenditures are necessary.

The structure: The cash budget consists of four major sections:
- The *receipts* section, including beginning cash balance, cash collections from customers, and other receipts.
- The *disbursements* section, comprising all cash payments made by purpose.
- The *cash surplus or deficit* section, showing the difference between the cash receipts section and the cash disbursements section.
- The *financing* section, providing a detailed account of the borrowings and repayments expected during the budgeting period.

Key 18   Financial forecasting and the percent-of-sales method

OVERVIEW   *Financial forecasting, an essential element of planning, is the basis for budgeting. Forecasts of future sales and their related expenses provide the firm with the information needed to project future financing needs.*

Financial forecasting: The basic steps in projecting financing needs are:
1. Project the firm's sales. The sales forecast is the initial step; most other forecasts (budgets) follow the sales forecast.
2. Project additional variables, such as expenses.
3. Estimate the level of investment in current and fixed assets required to support the projected sales.
4. Calculate the firm's financing needs.

The percent-of-sales method: estimates expenses, assets, and liabilities for a future period as a percent of the sales forecast and then, using these percentages together with projected sales, constructs pro forma balance sheets. The computational steps are:
1. Express those balance-sheet items (asset and liability accounts) that vary directly with sales as a percentage of sales. Any item such as long-term debt that does not vary directly with sales is designated ''n.a.''or ''not applicable.''
2. Multiply these percentages by projected sales.
3. Insert figures for long-term debt, common stock, and paid-in-capital from the current balance sheet.
4. Compute the new retained earnings after calculating projected net income less planned dividends.
5. Project the firm's financing needs as the projected level of total assets less projected liabilities and equity.

Advantages: Simple and inexpensive to use.

Assumption: The firm is operating at full capacity.

Theme 4 THE MANAGEMENT OF ASSETS

*T*he management of working capital involves regulating current assets and current liabilities to achieve a proper balance in terms of risk and return. Cash management attempts to accelerate cash inflow to obtain a return while delaying cash payments. Various cash models may be used to derive the optimal cash position based on corporate needs. Excess cash may be invested temporarily in a host of different marketable securities. Managing accounts receivable includes deciding the amount and terms of credit to be given to customers. If collections are accelerated, the company's cash flow and profitability benefit. Inventory management involves determining the optimum amount to order each time in order to minimize total inventory costs while avoiding stockouts that lead to lost sales.

Key 19 Working capital management

OVERVIEW *Working capital is equal to current assets. Net working capital equals current assets less current liabilities. The management of working capital involves regulating the various current assets and current liabilities.*

Characteristics: Management of net working capital requires deciding how to finance current assets—through short-term debt, long-term debt, or equity capital.
- Net working capital is increased when current assets are financed through noncurrent sources.
- The liquidity of current assets affects the terms and availability of short-term credit.

Risk-return trade-off: holding more current assets than fixed assets means:
- A reduced liquidity risk
- Greater flexibility, since current assets may be modified easily as sales volume changes. However, the rate of return is typically less with current assets than with fixed assets.
- Long-term financing has less liquidity risk than short-term debt, but it also carries a higher cost.

Financing:
- Short-term debt rather than long-term financing is best for buying seasonal inventory. Short-term debt gives the firm flexibility to meet seasonal needs within its ability to repay the loan.
- Long-term debt is used to finance permanent assets.
- The *hedging approach* to financing (financing assets with liabilities of similar maturity) is wise.

Key 20   Cash management

OVERVIEW   *Cash refers to currency and demand deposits. Cash management involves having the optimum amount of cash on hand at the right time. The company should know how much cash it needs, how much it has, where the cash is, what its sources are, and how much can be spent.*

Factors in determining the cash level: 1. liquidity position, 2. schedule of debt maturity, 3. ability to borrow and how much time is required, 4. expected cash flow, 5. risk preferences, and 6. line of credit.
  - A smaller cash balance may be maintained when cash receipts and cash payments are highly synchronized and predictable.

Cash management system: feasible if the return earned on the freed cash exceeds the cost of the system, such as bank charges and office staff salaries.
  - Analyze each bank account as to type, balance and cost.

Acceleration of cash inflow:
  - Accelerate billing and deposit checks quickly.
  - Charge interest on delinquent accounts receivable balances.
  - Send customers preaddressed, stamped envelopes.
  - Require deposits on large or custom orders or progress payments.
  - Offer discounts for early payment.
  - Have postdated checks from customers.
  - Have cash-on-delivery terms.
  - Avoid tying up cash unnecessarily in other accounts, such as advances to employees.

Lockbox and concentration banking: Have the collection center located near the customer, such as lockboxes at strategic post offices. The local bank collects from these lockboxes periodically during the day.
  - Since the lockbox system usually has a significant per-item cost, it is most cost-effective with low-volume, high-dollar remissions.
  - Before implementing a lockbox system, do a cost-benefit analysis including: 1. average dollar amount of checks received, 2. potential savings, 3. processing cost, and 4. reduction in mailing time per check.

- Use concentration banking in which funds are collected by several local banks and transferred to a main concentration account in another bank. The transfer of funds may be accomplished through depository transfer checks (DTCs) or wire transfers.

Delay of cash outflow:
- Centralize the payable operation so that debt may be paid at the most profitable time.
- Make partial payments.
- Use payment drafts on which payment is not made on demand.
- Draw checks on banks in distant locations.
- Mail payments from post offices with limited service or in which mail has to go through several handling points.
- Use probability analysis to determine the expected dates for checks to clear.
- Use a computer to transfer funds between various bank accounts at opportune times.
- Use a charge account to lengthen the time between buying goods or services and paying for them.
- Do not pay bills before due dates.
- Delay the frequency of company payrolls.
- Disburse commissions on sales when the receivables are collected rather than when the sales are made.

Key 21 Cash management models

OVERVIEW *Cash models may be used to determine the optimal cash balance considering costs, return rate, and fluctuations in cash flow.*

William Baumol Model: a model to determine the optimum amount of transaction cash under conditions of certainty. The objective is to minimize the sum of the fixed costs associated with transactions and the opportunity cost of holding cash balances. Costs are expressed

as: $F \frac{(T)}{2} + i \frac{(C)}{2}$

where F = the fixed cost of a transaction
   T = the total cash needed for the time period
   i = the interest rate on marketable securities
   C = cash balance

- The optimal level of cash equals: $C = \sqrt{\dfrac{2FT}{i}}$

Miller-Orr model: a stochastic approach used when uncertainty exists regarding cash payments.

- The model places upper and lower limits for cash balances.
- When the upper limit is reached, a transfer of cash to marketable securities is made.
- When the lower limit is reached, a transfer from marketable securities to cash occurs.
- No transaction takes place as long as the cash balance falls within the limits.

- The optimal cash balance Z is computed: $Z = \sqrt[3]{\dfrac{3F\sigma^2}{4i}} + LL$

   where F = fixed cost of a securities transaction assumed to be the same for buying and selling
      i = the daily interest rate on marketable securities
      σ^2 = the variability of daily net cash flows
      LL = the actual value for the lower limit

- LL is set by management
- Upper control limit, UL, can be computed: $UL = 3Z - 2LL$
- The objective of the model is to meet cash requirements at the lowest possible cost.

Key 22   Marketable securities

OVERVIEW   *Marketable securities are readily tradeable debt or equity securities with quoted prices. They are near-cash assets and are classified under current assets since the intent is to hold them for one year or less. Examples of liquid securities are treasury bills, commercial paper, certificates of deposit, and money market funds.*

Investing in marketable securities:
- Excess cash may be invested in marketable securities for a return. *Example:* Seasonal companies may buy marketable securities when they have excess funds and then sell the securities when cash deficits occur.
- Holding marketable securities serves as protection against cash shortages.
- Funds may be held temporarily in marketable securities in expectation of short-term capital expansion.
- In selecting marketable securities, consider return, safety, default risk, marketability, and maturity date.

Key 23 Management of accounts receivable

OVERVIEW *The management of accounts receivable improves the company's cash flow and profitability. There is an opportunity cost of holding receivable balances. Determining the amount and terms of credit to extend to customers is a major management decision.*

Credit policy: Credit terms impact the costs of and revenue from receivables.

- If credit terms are tight, the investment in accounts receivable will be smaller and there will be fewer bad debts, but there will be lower sales and reduced profitability.
- If credit terms are liberal, there will be more sales and increased profitability, but there will be a larger investment in accounts receivable and more bad debts.
- Avoid typically high-risk receivables (e.g., customers in a financially troubled industry).
- Revise credit limits as the customer's financial position changes.
- Offer more liberal payment terms in slow seasons to stimulate sales.
- Ask for collateral in support of questionable accounts.
- Determine average accounts receivable balance equal to:

$$\frac{\text{Days outstanding} \times \text{Annual credit sales}}{360}$$

Billing policy: Set your billing cycle to produce uniformity.

- Mail customer statements one day after the end of the accounting period.
- Bill large sales immediately.
- Invoice customers for goods when the order is processed instead of when it is shipped.

Collection policy: Initiate collection efforts when the first signs of a customer's financial problems are evident.

- Age accounts receivable to identify delinquent customers. Compare aging to industry norms, competitors, and prior years.
- Compare the credit terms to the length of time the receivables are uncollectible.

- Use collection agencies when warranted.
- Have credit insurance to guard against unusual bad-debt losses.

Special decision: Offer a discount for early payment by customers when the return on the funds received exceeds the cost of the discount.

- In determining whether to offer credit to higher-than-normal risk customers, consider:
- Profitability on additional sales generated versus additional bad debts, higher investigation and collection costs, and the opportunity cost of tying up funds in receivables.
- When there is idle capacity, the additional profit is the incremental contribution margin (sales less variable cost), because fixed costs are constant. The incremental investment in receivables equals:

$$\text{Average accounts receivable} \times \frac{\text{Unit cost}}{\text{Unit selling price}}$$

Key 24 Inventory management

OVERVIEW *Inventory management is a trade-off between the costs of keeping inventory* versus *the benefits of holding it. High inventory levels result in increased carrying costs but lower the possibility of sales lost because of stockouts and production slowdowns resulting from inadequate stocking.*

Types of inventory: *raw materials* (materials acquired from a supplier to be used in the manufacture of goods), *work-in-process* (partially completed goods), and *finished goods* (completed goods ready for sale).

Inventory management practices:
- Appraise adequacy of raw material levels.
- If prices of raw materials are expected to sharply increase, buy more now.
- Discard slow-moving items to reduce carrying costs and improve cash flow.
- Watch out for inventory buildup.
- Minimize inventory levels when cash flow and liquidity problems exist.
- Examine the quality of merchandise received.
- Monitor backorders, since a high backorder level indicates a reduced need for inventory.
- Evaluate internal inventory control.
- Minimize lead time in the acquisition, manufacturing, and distribution functions.
- Examine the degree of spoilage or obsolescence.
- Appraise high inventory risk items, such as technological, perishable, fashionable, flammable, and specialized goods.

Inventory costs:
- *Carrying cost:* cost of holding inventory (storage, handling, insurance, spoilage, property taxes, and opportunity cost).

$$\text{Carrying cost} = \frac{Q}{2} \times C$$

where $\frac{Q}{2}$ = average quantity

C = cost of carrying one unit in stock

- *Ordering cost:* cost to place the order and receive the merchandise.

$$\text{Ordering cost} = \frac{S}{Q} \times O$$

where S = usage
Q = quantity per order
O = cost of placing one order
- Total Inventory Cost = Carrying Cost + Ordering Cost

$$\left(\frac{Q}{2} \times C\right) + \left(\frac{S}{Q} \times O\right)$$

- A trade-off exists between ordering and carrying costs. A greater order quantity increases carrying costs but lowers ordering costs.

Economic order quantity (EOQ): optimum amount of goods to order each time to minimize total inventory costs.

$$EOQ = \sqrt{\frac{2SO}{C}}$$

Safety stock: extra units of inventory carried as protection against possible stockouts, based on expected usage and anticipated delivery time.

Stockout Cost = Number of orders × stockout units × unit stockout cost × probability of a stockout

Reorder point: the level of inventory that signals the time to reorder merchandise at the EOQ amount.

Reorder Point = Lead time in weeks × weekly usage + safety stock

ABC inventory control method: system of classifying inventory into groups A, B, or C. Group A items are the most expensive and require the greatest control, while Group C items are the least expensive and require the least control.

Theme 5 RISK, RETURN, AND VALUATION

*C*ompanies face many risks, including business risk, liquidity risk, default risk, market risk, interest rate risk, and purchasing power risk. Portfolio risk may be reduced through diversification. Models have been developed dealing with the risk and return of portfolios. Beta, the percentage change in the price of a company's stock relative to the change in a stock market index, is a measure of the risk of a company's stock. Return is in the form of current income and appreciation in the price of a security. However, a risk-return trade-off exists in that achieving a greater return requires taking increased risk. Several approaches to bond and stock valuation need to be considered.

Key 25 Risk

OVERVIEW *Risk refers to the variability of cash flow (or earnings) around the expected value (return) and can be measured in either absolute or relative terms. Statistics such as standard deviation and coefficient of variation are used to measure risk.*

Standard deviation and coefficient of variation:
1. First, the expected value $\overline{A}$ is

$$\overline{A} = \sum_{i=1}^{n} A_i\, P_i$$

where A_i = the value of the ith possible outcome
P_i = the probability that the ith outcome will occur
n = the number of possible outcomes
2. Then, the absolute risk is measured by the standard deviation:
   a. Subtract each possible outcome from the expected value $\overline{A}$.
   b. Square the deviations $(A - \overline{A})$.
   c. Multiply the squared deviations $[(A - \overline{A})^2]$ by the associated probability.
   d. Determine the square root.

$$\sigma = \sqrt{\sum (A_i - \overline{A})^2\, P_i}$$

3. The relative risk is measured by the coefficient of variation, which is $\sigma/\overline{A}$

Sources of risk: Financial managers must consider the following types of risk:
- *Business risk:* depends on variability in demand, sales price, input prices, and amount of operating leverage; causes fluctuations in operating income.
- *Liquidity risk:* possibility that an asset may not be readily sold on short notice for its market value. If an investment must be sold at a high discount, then it is said to have a substantial amount of liquidity risk.
- *Default risk:* risk that a borrower will be unable to make interest payments or principal repayments on debt. There is a great amount

of default risk inherent in the bonds of a company experiencing financial difficulty.

- *Market risk:* changes in a stock's price that result from changes in the stock market as a whole, regardless of the fundamental change in a firm's earning power. Prices of all stocks are correlated to some degree with broad swings in the stock market.
- *Interest-rate risk:* fluctuations in the value of an asset as the interest rates and conditions of the money and capital markets change. Interest-rate risk relates to fixed-income securities such as bonds. *Example:* If interest rates rise (fall), bond prices fall (rise).
- *Purchasing-power risk:* possibility that an investor will receive a lesser amount of purchasing power than was originally invested. Bonds are affected most by this risk, since the issuer repays principal in cheaper dollars during an inflationary period.

Key 26   Portfolio theory

OVERVIEW   *Most financial assets are not held in isolation. What is important is the expected return on the portfolio (not just the return on one asset) and the portfolio's risk.*

Portfolio return: The expected return on a portfolio (r_p) is the weighted average return of the individual securities in the portfolio, the weights being the fraction of the total funds invested in each asset.

The formula is: $r_p = w_1r_1 + w_2r_2 + \ldots + w_nr_n$
$$= \Sigma\ w_jr_j$$

where the r_j's are the expected returns in individual securities, the w's are the fractions, n is the number of assets in the portfolio, and $\Sigma\ w_j = 1.0$.

Portfolio risk: Unlike returns, the riskiness of a portfolio (σp) is *not* simply a weighted average of the standard deviations of the individual securities in the portfolio.

- In a two-asset portfolio, portfolio risk is defined as:

$$\sigma_p = \sqrt{w_A^2\sigma_A^2 + w_B^2\sigma_B^2 + 2\ w_Aw_B \cdot \rho_{AB} \cdot \sigma_A\sigma_B}$$

    where σ_A and σ_B are the standard deviations of the possible returns from security A and security B, respectively, w_A and w_B are the weights of fractions of total funds invested in security A and security B, and ρ_{AB} is the correlation coefficient between security A and security B. The correlation coefficient is the measurement of joint movement between two securities.

Diversification: a way to minimize portfolio risk. Such a risk reduction depends upon the correlation between the assets being combined.

- Generally speaking, by combining two perfectly negatively correlated assets ($\rho = -1.0$), you can eliminate the risk completely. In the real world, however, most securities are negatively, but not perfectly, correlated.

Markowitz's efficient portfolio: assumes rational investors behave in a way that reflects their aversion to taking increased risk without being compensated by an adequate increase in expected return.

- For any given expected return, most investors prefer a lower risk; for any given level of risk, most investors prefer a higher return.
- Investors try to find the optimum portfolio by using the indifference curve, which shows the trade-off between risk and return.

Key 27   Market index models

OVERVIEW   *The number of data inputs for even a moderate-size portfolio using the Markowitz portfolio selection model can be staggering. William Sharpe developed a model, called the market index (or single-index) model, that drastically reduced the data requirements necessary to perform portfolio analysis.*

Market index model: Sharpe suggests that all securities are linearly related to a market index. This relationship can be expressed through the equation:

$$r_j = a + b\ r_m + u_j$$

where a = alpha and b = beta, the index of systematic risk that represents the individual securities' relationship with the market. The random error u_j represents the unsystematic or nonmarket-related return of an individual asset.

- Beta is measured as follows:

$$b = \frac{\text{Cov}\ (r_j, r_m)}{\sigma_m^2}$$

where Cov (r_j, r_m) = the covariance of the returns of the securities with the market return and σ_m^2 = the variance (standard deviation squared) of the market return.
- Securities are assumed to be related to one another through their relationship with the market.
- Rather than computing the covariances of all combinations of securities in a portfolio, the Sharpe model assumes that all securities are related to one another through their relationship with a market index such as the Standard & Poor's 500 Index or Dow Jones 30 Industrials.

Key 28 Capital asset pricing model
(CAPM)

OVERVIEW *The capital asset pricing model (CAPM) relates the risk measured by beta to the level of expected or required rate of return on a security. The model, also called the security market line (SML), is a general relationship to show the risk-return trade-off for an individual security.*

The security market line: The model of SML is:

$$r_j = r_f + b\,(r_m - r_f)$$

where r_j = the expected (or required) return on
security j
r_f = the risk-free security (such as a T-bill)
r_m = the expected return on the market portfolio
(such as Standard & Poor's 500 Stock Composite
Index or Dow Jones 30 Industrials)
b = Beta, an index of nondiversifiable (uncontrollable,
systematic) risk

- The term $b(r_m - r_f)$ represents the risk premium, the additional return required to compensate investors for assuming a given level of risk.
- The CAPM or SML equation shows that the required or expected rate of return on a given security (r_j) is equal to the return required for securities that have no risk (r_f) plus a risk premium required by investors for assuming a given level of risk.
- The higher the degree of systematic risk (b), the higher the return on a given security demanded by investors.

What does the capital asset pricing model (CAPM) mean? The model shows that investors in individual securities are assumed to be rewarded for systematic, uncontrollable, market-related risk, known as the beta (b) risk. All other risks are assumed to be diversified and thus are not rewarded.

Key 29 Beta

OVERVIEW   *Unsystematic risk is unique to a given security and can be controlled through diversification. Nondiversifiable risk, commonly referred to as systematic risk (beta), results from forces outside the firm's control and is therefore not unique to the given security. Purchasing power, interest rate, and market risks fall into this category, measured by beta.*

Use of beta: measures a security's volatility relative to an average security. Beta helps to figure out risk and expected return.

KEY CONCEPT

How to read beta:

Beta	*What It Means*
0	The security's return is independent of the market. An example is a risk-free security such as a T-bill.
0.5	The security is only half as responsive as the market.
1.0	The security has the same risk as the market (i.e., average risk). This is the beta value of market portfolios such as Standard & Poor's 500 or the Dow Jones 30 Industrials.
2.0	The security is twice as responsive, or risky, as the market.

Example: If ABC's beta is 2.0, and the stock market goes up 10%, ABC's common stock goes up 20%; if the market drops 10%, ABC drops 20%.

How to measure beta: Compute beta by determining the slope of the least-squares linear regression line $(r_j - r_f)$, where the excess return of the asset $(r_j - r_f)$ is regressed against the excess return of the market portfolio $(r_m - r_f)$.

- The formula for b is: $b = \dfrac{\Sigma\, MK - n\, \overline{M}\, \overline{K}}{\Sigma\, M^2 - n\, \overline{M}^2}$

  where $M = (r_m - r_f)$
  $K = (r_j - r_f)$
  n = number of years
  $\overline{M}$ = average of M
  $\overline{K}$ = average of K

- Beta also may be determined using William Sharpe's Market Index Model. See Key 27.

Key 30 Return

OVERVIEW *Return is the reward for investing. It consists of the following sources of income:*
- *Periodic cash payments, called current income.*
- *Appreciation (or depreciation) in market value, called capital gains (or losses).*

Current income: includes interest, dividends, and rent; is received on a periodic basis.

Capital gains or losses: changes in market value.
- A capital gain is the amount by which the proceeds from the sale of an investment exceed the original purchase price. If the investment is sold for less than its purchase price, then the difference is a capital loss.

Holding period return (HPR): total return earned from holding an investment for a given period of time.

$$HPR = \frac{\text{Current income} + \text{Capital gain (or loss)}}{\text{Purchase price}}$$

- In the case of stock, we use the following symbols:

$$r = \frac{D_1 + (P_1 - P_0)}{P_0}$$

where r = expected return for a single period
   D_1 = dividend at the end of the period
   P_1 = price per share at the end of the period
   P_0 = price per share at the beginning of the period

Key 31   The risk-return trade-off

OVERVIEW   *All financial decisions involve some sort of risk-return trade-off. The greater the risk associated with any financial or investment decision, the greater the return expected from it.*

Connection with inventory: The less inventory a firm keeps, the higher the expected return (because less of the firm's current assets are tied up). But there is also a greater risk of running out of stock and thus losing potential revenue.

Trade-off: The investor must compare the expected return from a given investment with the risk associated with it. Generally speaking, the higher the risk undertaken, the more ample the return; conversely, the lower the risk, the more modest the return. *Example:* Investors demand higher return from a speculative stock to compensate for the higher level of risk.

Policy: Proper assessment and balance of the various risk-return trade-offs is part of creating a sound financial and investment plan.

Key 32   Bond valuation

OVERVIEW   *The process of determining bond valuation involves finding the present value of a bond's expected future cash flows, using the investor's required rate of return.*

Basic security valuation model:

$$V = \sum_{t=1}^{n} \frac{C_t}{(1 + r)^t}$$

where V = intrinsic value or present value of an asset
C_t = expected future cash flows in period $t = 1, \ldots, n$
r = investor's required rate of return

Bond valuation: includes three basic elements: 1. the amount of the cash flows to be received, which is equal to the total of the periodic interest and the maturity value; 2. the maturity date of the loan; and 3. the investor's required rate of return.

• If the interest payments are made annually, then

$$V = \sum_{t=1}^{n} \frac{I}{(1 + r)^t} + \frac{M}{(1 + r)^n} = I(\text{PVIFA}_{r,n}) + M(\text{PVIF}_{r,n})$$

where I = interest payment each year = coupon interest
rate × par value
M = par value, or maturity value, typically \$1,000
r = investor's required rate of return
n = number of years to maturity
PVIFA = present value interest factor of an annuity of \$1
PVIF = present value interest factor of \$1

• If the interest is paid semiannually, then

$$V = \sum_{t=1}^{2n} \frac{I/2}{(1 + r/2)^t} + \frac{M}{(1 + r/2)^{2n}} = \frac{I}{2}(\text{PVIFA}_{r/2,2n}) + M(\text{PVIF}_{r/2,2n})$$

Bond prices and interest rates: Bond prices and interest rates are inversely related. As interest rates rise, bond prices fall because investors can earn a greater return elsewhere. Further, increasing interest rates means lower corporate profitability, adversely affecting the market value of corporate securities.

Bond discount or premium: The yield on a bond must be compared to its nominal (coupon) interest rate.

- A bond will sell at par (usually $1,000) when its coupon (nominal) rate equals the going interest rate (or yield).
- The bond will sell at a discount from its face value if the yield is above the coupon rate.
- The bond will sell at a premium above its face value when the yield is below the coupon rate.

Key 33 Bond yield—effective rate of return on a bond

OVERVIEW *The bond yield is the effective interest rate earned on a bond. Returns or yields include current yield, yield to maturity (YTM), yield to call, and realized yield.*

Current yield: annual interest payment divided by the current price of the bond. The problem with this measure of return is that it does not take into account the maturity date of the bond.

Yield to maturity: real return to be received from interest income plus capital gain assuming the bond is held to maturity. Two computational methods are:

- *Exact method:* A bond's yield is the internal rate of return on the bond's investment. It is calculated by solving the bond valuation model for r:

$$V = \sum_{t=1}^{n} \frac{I}{(1+r)^t} + \frac{M}{(1+r)^n} = I(PVIFA_{r,n}) + M(PVIF_{r,n})$$

where V is the market price of the bond, I is the interest payment, and M is the maturity value, usually $1,000. Finding the bond's yield r involves trial and error.

- Approximate method:

$$\text{Yield} = \frac{I + (M-V)/n}{(M+V)/2}$$

where V = the market value of the bond
I = dollars of interest paid per year
M = maturity (face) value, usually $1,000
n = number of years to maturity

Yield to call: If the bond may be called prior to maturity, the yield to maturity formula uses the call price in place of the par value ($1,000).

Realized yield: Bondholders, who may trade in and out of a bond long before it matures, need a measure of return to evaluate the investment appeal of any bonds they intend to buy or sell. A variation of yield to maturity, with two variables changed: Future price is used in place of par value ($1,000), and the length of the holding period is substituted for the number of years to maturity.

Equivalent before-tax yield: yield on a tax-free municipal bond calculated on an equivalent before-tax yield basis (that is, what the equivalent yield would have to be on a taxable investment to have the same net yield after taxes).

$$\text{Tax equivalent yield} = \frac{\text{Tax-exempt yield}}{(1 - \text{tax rate})}$$

Example: A 7% municipal bond with a tax rate of 28% has an equivalent tax yield of 9.7% computed as follows:

$$\frac{.07}{(1 - .28)} = \frac{.07}{.72} = 9.7\%$$

Key 34 Term structure of interest rates

OVERVIEW *The term structure of interest rates, also known as a yield curve, shows the relationship between length of time to maturity and yields of debt instruments when other factors, such as default risk and tax treatment, are held constant.*

Importance: An understanding of the relationship between maturity and yield is important to financial managers who must decide whether to borrow by issuing long- or short-term debt.
* Fixed-income analysts should investigate the yield curve to project future interest rates.

Yield curve: a graphical presentation of the term structure of interest rates. It may take any number of shapes—flat (vertical), positive (ascending), inverted (descending), or humped (ascending and then descending).

Expectation theory: The shape of the yield curve reflects investors' expectations about future short-term rates.
* Given the estimated set of future short-term interest rates, the long-term rate is then established as the geometric average of future interest rates.
* A positive (ascending) yield curve implies that investors expect short-term rates to rise; a descending (inverted) yield curve implies that they expect short-term rates to fall.

Liquidity preference theory: contends that risk-averse investors prefer short-term bonds to long-term bonds, because long-term bonds have a greater chance of price variation.
* Current long-term bonds should include a liquidity premium as additional compensation for assuming interest-rate risk.

Market segmentation (preferred habitat) theory: does not recognize expectations and emphasizes the rigidity in loan allocation patterns by lenders. Interest rates are determined by supply and demand.

Key 35   Common stock valuation

OVERVIEW   *The process of determining common stock valuation involves finding the present value of its expected future cash flows, using the investor's required rate of return.*

Security valuation model:

$$V = \sum_{t=1}^{n} \frac{C_t}{(1+r)^t}$$

where V = intrinsic value or present value of an asset
C_t = expected future cash flows in period $t = 1, \ldots, n$
r = investor's required rate of return

Common stock valuation: the present value of all future cash inflows expected to be received by the investor, including dividends and future selling price.

Single holding period: For an investor holding a common stock for only one year, the value of the stock is the present value of both the expected cash dividend to be received in one year (D_1) and the expected market price per share of the stock at year-end (P_1).

If r represents an investor's required rate of return, the value of common stock (P_o) is:

$$P_o = \frac{D_1}{(1+r)^1} + \frac{P_1}{(1+r)^1}$$

Multiple holding period: Since common stock has no maturity date and is often held for many years, a more general, multiperiod model is needed. The general common stock valuation model is defined as follows:

$$P_o = \sum_{t=1}^{\infty} \frac{D_t}{(1+r)^t}$$

- The model is based on the concept that a common stock is worth the present value of future dividends. However, future dividends may follow three different patterns: zero growth, constant growth, or nonconstant (supernormal) growth.

Zero growth model: If dividends are expected to remain unchanged, the above model reduces to the formula:

$$P_o = \frac{D_1}{r}$$

- This is the case with a perpetuity. This model is most applicable to preferred stocks or the common stocks of very mature companies such as utilities.

Constant growth model: If dividends are assumed to grow at a constant rate of g every year, the above model is simplified to:

$$P_o = \frac{D_1}{r - g}$$

- This formula, known as the Gordon's dividend growth model, is most applicable to common stock of very large or broadly diversified companies.

Nonconstant, or supernormal, growth model: Firms typically go through life cycles; their growth rate may exceed that of the economy and then may fall sharply.

- the value of stock during supernormal growth can be calculated as follows: 1. Compute the dividends during the period of supernormal growth and find their present value, 2. find the price of the stock at the end of the supernormal growth period and compute its present value, and 3. add these two present value figures to find the value (P_o) of the common stock.

Price-earnings ratio—a pragmatic approach: forecasted price at the end of year = estimated EPS in year t × estimated P-E ratio.

Theme 6 TIME VALUE OF MONEY AND CAPITAL BUDGETING

When making an investment, consider the time value of money; the longer it takes to receive a dollar, the less it will be worth in today's dollars. Capital budgeting is the selection of the optimum alternative long-term investment opportunity. There are many capital budgeting methods, including the return on the investment, the payback period (how long it takes to recoup the initial investment), net present value, and internal rate of return. In some cases, proposals are mutually exclusive; the acceptance of one precludes the acceptance of the other. When budget constraints exist, capital rationing is required. Inflation and risk must also be taken into account in investment selection.

Key 36 Time value of money and its applications

OVERVIEW *Time value of money is a critical consideration in financial decisions. Compound interest calculations determine future sums of money that will result from an investment. Discounting, or the calculation of present value, is inversely related to compounding. It is used to evaluate future cash flow associated with capital budgeting projects.*

Future values—compounding: A dollar on hand today is worth more than a dollar to be received tomorrow because of the interest it could earn.

- Compounding interest means that interest earns interest.
- For the discussion of the concepts of compounding and time value, let us define:

  F_n = future value = the amount of money at the end of year n
  P = principal
  i = annual interest rate
  n = number of years

  Then, F_1 = the amount of money at the end of year 1
  $\qquad\quad$ = principal and interest
  $\qquad\quad$ = $P + iP = P(1 + i)$
  $\quad\ \ F_2$ = the amount of money at the end of year 2
  $\qquad\quad$ = $F_1 (1 + i) = P (1 + i) (1 + i) = P (1 + i)^2$

The future value of an investment compounded annually at rate i for n years is

$$F_n = P (1 + i)^n = P \cdot FVIF_{i,n}$$

where $FVIF_{i,n}$ is the future value interest factor for $1.

Future value of an annuity: a series of year-end payments (or receipts) of a fixed amount of money for a specified number of periods.

KEY EQUATION

Let S_n = the future value on an n-year annuity

 A = the amount of an annuity

Then we can write

$$S_n = A(1 + i)^{n-1} + A(1 + i)^{n-2} + \ldots + A(1 + i)^0$$
$$= A[(i + i)^{n-1} + (1 + i)^{n-2} + \ldots + (1 + i)^0]$$
$$= A \cdot \sum_{t=0}^{n-1} (1 + i)^t$$
$$= A \left[\frac{[(1.0 + i)^n - 1.0]}{i} \right] = A. \text{ FVIFA}_{i,n}$$

where $\text{FVIFA}_{i,n}$ represents the future value interest factor for an n-year annuity compounded at i percent.

Present value—discounting: present worth of future sums of money.

- The process of calculating present values, or discounting, is actually the opposite of finding the compounded future value. In connection with present value calculations, the interest rate i is called the discount rate.
- Recall that $\quad F_n = P (1 + i)^n$

  Therefore,

$$P = \frac{F_n}{(1 + i)^n} = F_n \left[\frac{1}{(1 + i)^n} \right] = F_n \cdot \text{PVIF}_{i,n}$$

where $\text{PVIF}_{i,n}$ represents the present value interest factor for \$1.

Present value of mixed streams of cash flow: The present value of a series of mixed payments (or receipts) is the sum of the present value of each individual payment. The present value of each individual payment is the payment times the appropriate PVIF.

Present value of an annuity: present worth of receiving equal year-end annual payments.

- Interest received from bonds, pension funds, and insurance obligations all involve annuities.

KEY EQUATION

The present value of an annuity (P_n) can be found by using the following equation:

$$P_n = A \cdot \frac{1}{(1 + i)^1} + A \cdot \frac{1}{(1 = i)^2} + \ldots + A \cdot \frac{1}{(1 = i)^n}$$

$$= A\left[\frac{1}{(1 + i)^1} + \frac{1}{(1 + i)^2} + \ldots + \frac{1}{(1 + i)^n}\right]$$

$$= A \cdot \sum_{t=1}^{n} \frac{1}{(1 + i)^t}$$

$$= A \cdot \frac{\left[1.0 - \dfrac{1.0}{(1.0 + i)^n}\right]}{i} = A \cdot PVIFA_{i,n}$$

where $PVIFA_{i,n}$ represents the appropriate value for the present value interest factor for a \$1 annuity discounted at i percent for n years.

Perpetuities: annuities that go on forever. *Example:* Preferred stock which yields a constant dollar dividend indefinitely.

Some applications of future values and present values: future savings in a bank account; annual payment on a loan; annual deposit in an investment account; growth rate in earnings; rate of return; periods needed to accumulate a desired amount in a sinking fund; price to be paid for an investment; accumulated amount in a pension plan. *Example:* To find the annual deposit (or payment) necessary to accumulate a future sum, use the following formula:

$$S_n = A. \, FVIFA_{i,n}$$

Solving for A, we obtain:

$$\text{Sinking fund amount} = A = \frac{Sn}{FVIFA_{i,n}}$$

Key 37   Capital budgeting

OVERVIEW   *Capital budgeting is the process of deciding whether to commit resources to a project whose benefits will be spread over several time periods. Capital budgeting decisions are a key factor in the long-term profitability of a firm. To make wise investment decisions, financial managers need tools to guide them in comparing the benefits and costs of various investment alternatives.*

Types of investment decisions:
- Selection decisions in terms of obtaining new facilities or expanding existing facilities. *Examples:* Purchase of equipment; new product development.
- Replacement decisions concerning existing facilities.

Income tax considerations: A project that is attractive on a pre-tax basis may have to be rejected on an after-tax basis. Income taxes typically affect both the amount and the timing of cash flows.

Types of cash flows: An investment's cash flows fall into three categories:
- The initial investment
- The incremental projected cash flows over the investment's life
- The terminal cash flow

Incremental (differential) cash flow: The incremental cash flow generated by a project involves the after-tax cash flows that result from increased revenues and/or savings in operating expenses.
- It includes the depreciation tax shield on an incremental basis in replacement decisions.
- It does not include interest expense if the project is financed by debt; this is accounted for in the cost of capital.

Capital budgeting techniques:
- Accounting rate of return
- Payback period
- Net present value
- Profitability index
- Internal rate of return. See Keys 38 to 42.

Key 38   Accounting rate of return

OVERVIEW *Accounting rate of return (ARR), also called simple rate of return, book rate of return, or unadjusted rate of return, measures profitability by relating the required investment to the future annual net income.*

Decision rule: Choose the project with the higher rate of return.

Two versions of ARR:
- Using the initial investment:

$$ARR = \frac{\text{Expected future annual net income}}{\text{Required initial investment}}$$

- Using the average investment (result called average rate of return):

$$\frac{\text{Expected future annual net income}}{\text{Average investment}}$$

- The average investment is typically considered to be one-half of the original investment. As a result, the average rate of return is twice the ARR.

Advantages:
- Easily understandable and simple to compute
- Recognizes the profitability factor

Disadvantages:
- Ignores the time value of money
- Uses accounting data instead of cash flow data

Key 39 Payback period

OVERVIEW *The payback period is the length of time required to recover the initial capital investment.*

Calculation: If the cash inflows are uniform:

$$\text{Payback period} = \frac{\text{Initial investment}}{\text{Annual cash inflows}}$$

- If annual cash inflows are not even, the payback period must be determined by trial and error.

Payback reciprocal: reciprocal of the payback time. It gives a quick, accurate estimate of the internal rate of return (IRR) on an investment when the project life is more than twice the payback period and the cash inflows are uniform every period.

Decision rule: Choose the project with the shorter payback period because there is greater liquidity and less risk.

Advantages:
- Is simple to compute and easy to understand
- Handles investment risk effectively

Disadvantages:
- Ignores profitability of an investment
- Does not recognize the time value of money

Discounted payback period: the length of time required to recover the initial cash outflow from the *discounted* future cash inflows. This is obtained when the present values of cash inflows add up to equal the initial investment.

Key 40   Net present value method

OVERVIEW   *The net present value (NPV) method is a discounted cash flow technique widely used for evaluating investment projects. Under the NPV method, the present value (PV) of all cash inflows from the project is compared to the initial investment (I).*

Calculation:
1. The future net cash flows from the project are *discounted* to their present value at an appropriate discount rate (the project's *cost of capital*).
2. The initial cost of the project is then subtracted from the present value to determine the NPV.

Decision rule: If the net present value is positive (NPV > 0 or PV > I), the project should be accepted. If it is negative, the project should be rejected.
- If two projects are *mutually exclusive*, the one with the higher NPV should be selected.

Advantages:
- Recognizes the time value of money
- Is relatively easy to calculate
- Ranks *mutually exclusive* investments
- Is consistent with stockholder wealth maximization as the firm's goal

Disadvantages:
- Is not as easily understood as the rate-of-return concept
- May not work well in *capital rationing* cases

Key 41   Profitability index

OVERVIEW   *Profitability index (PI) is an easily-comput-ed index that is widely used for ranking investment projects in terms of their relative attractiveness. The present value of future cash inflows from the project is expressed on a per-dollar invested basis.*

Definition: The PI is the ratio of the total present value (PV) of future cash inflows to the initial investment (I):

$$\frac{\text{PV of future cash inflows}}{\text{Initial investment}}$$

- It facilitates comparison of different size investments and puts all proposals on a comparative basis, eliminating the distorting effect of size.

Decision rule: In a single-project case, if the index is greater than 1, accept the project; otherwise reject it.

- This index is primarily used as a means of ranking projects in *capital rationing* situations.

Key 42   Internal rate of return (IRR)

OVERVIEW   *Internal rate of return (IRR) is the time-adjusted, real rate earned on a proposal.*

Computation: IRR is that rate of interest that equates the initial investment (I) with the present value (PV) of future cash inflows. That is, at IRR, I = PV, or NPV (net present value) = 0.
- The IRR method is easy to determine as long as cash inflows are even from year to year. If the cash flows are uneven, the IRR must be determined by trial and error.

Decision rule: Accept the project if IRR exceeds the cost of capital; otherwise reject the proposal.
- The IRR method ranks mutually exclusive investments differently from the NPV method if 1. the cost of one project is larger than the cost of the other, and 2. the timing of the project's cash flow differs over time.

KEY EXAMPLE

A company invests $100,000 in a proposal that will produce annual cash inflows of $15,000 a year for the next 20 years. The factor to obtain the IRR is 6.6667 ($100,000/$15,000). Looking at the present value of an annuity of $1 table (PVIFA) for n = 20 at a factor closest to 6.6667 (which is a factor of 6.6231) we find that the IRR is approximately 14%. Assuming the company's cost of capital is 10%, the project should be accepted.

Advantages:
- Is easily understood and has intuitive economic meaning
- Considers the time value of money and is therefore more exact and realistic than the *accounting rate of return*

Disadvantages:
- Can be tedious to calculate, especially when cash inflows are not even
- Fails to recognize the varying size of investment in competing projects
- If there are multiple reversals in the cash flow streams, the project may yield more than one internal rate of return

Key 43 Mutually exclusive investments

OVERVIEW *Projects are mutually exclusive if the acceptance of one automatically precludes the acceptance of one or more other projects. If you are choosing between mutually exclusive investments, the NPV and IRR methods may yield contradictory indications.*

Conditions for conflicting rankings:
- Projects with different life expectancies
- Projects with different sizes of investment
- Projects with differing cash flows over time. *Example:* The cash flows of one project increase over time, while those of another decrease.

Different reinvestment assumptions:
- The contradictions result from different assumptions with respect to the reinvestment rate on cash flows from the projects.
- The NPV method discounts all cash flows at the cost of capital, thus implicitly assuming that these cash flows can be reinvested at this rate.
- The IRR method implies a reinvestment rate at IRR. Thus, the implied reinvestment rate differs from project to project.
- The NPV method generally gives correct ranking, since the cost of capital is a more realistic reinvestment rate.

Some examples of mutually exclusive proposals:
- Selecting one geographic location for a new plant instead of another
- Deciding which machine type to buy
- Deciding whether to produce product X or product Y

Key 44   Lease-purchase decision

OVERVIEW   *The lease-purchase decision is a common one for companies considering the acquisition of new assets. It is a hybrid capital budgeting decision that forces a company to compare the leasing and purchasing alternatives. To make an intelligent decision, an after-tax cash outflow— present value comparison is needed.*

Steps to take when considering a lease:
1. Find the annual lease payment. Since the annual lease payment is typically made in advance, the formula to use is:

$$\text{Amount of lease} = A + A(\text{PVIFA}_{i,n-1}) \text{ or } A = \frac{\text{Amount of lease}}{1 + \text{PVIFA}_{i,n-1}}$$

Notice we use $n - 1$ rather than n.
2. Find the after-tax cash outflows.
3. Find the present value of the after-tax cash outflows.

Steps to take when considering a purchase:
1. Find the annual loan amortization by using:

$$A = \frac{\text{Amount of loan for the purchase}}{\text{PVIFA}_{i,n}}$$

This step may not be necessary since this amount is usually available.

2. Calculate the interest. The interest is segregated from the principal in each of the annual loan payments because only the interest is tax deductible.
3. Find the cash outflows by adding interest and depreciation (plus any maintenance costs), and then compute the after-tax outflows.
4. Find the present value of the after-tax cash outflows.

Key 45 Capital rationing

OVERVIEW *Many companies specify a limit on the overall capital spending budget. Capital rationing is concerned with selecting the mix of acceptable projects that provides the highest overall net present value (NPV).*

Decision rule: The profitability index (PI) is widely used in ranking projects competing for limited funds.
- Rank the projects in the descending order of PI.
- Then select projects from the list until the total amount of money available is exhausted.

Disadvantages:
- Breaks down whenever more than one resource is rationed.
- In addition to the capital budget constraint, there may be 1. labor shortages, 2. mutually exclusiveness, or 3. technical interdependency. In this case, the use of *zero-one programming* is suggested.

KEY EXAMPLE

Assume that a company has a fixed budget of $250,000 and must choose between the following projects:

Project	I	PV	PI	Ranking
A	$ 70,000	$112,000	1.6	1
B	100,000	145,000	1.45	2
C	110,000	126,500	1.15	4
D	60,000	79,000	1.32	3

Using the profitability index, we select projects A, B, and D:

	I	PV
A	$ 70,000	$112,000
B	100,000	145,000
D	60,000	79,000
	$230,000	$336,000

where NPV = $336,000 − $230,000 = $106,000

Key 46   Capital budgeting and inflation

OVERVIEW   *The accuracy of capital budgeting deci-sions depends on data reliability regarding cash inflows and outflows. For example, the failure to incorporate price-level changes in capital budgeting situations can result in errors in predicting cash flows and thus in incorrect decisions.*

Two approaches: Typically, a financial manager has two basically equivalent options for dealing with a capital budgeting situation involving inflation.
- Restate the cash flows in nominal terms and discount them at a nominal *cost of capital* (minimum required rate of return).
- Restate both the cash flows and cost of capital in constant terms and discount the constant cash flows at a constant cost of capital. Instead of converting the cash-flow forecasts into nominal terms, you can convert the cost of capital into real terms by using the following formula:

$$\text{Real cost of capital} = \frac{1 + \text{nominal cost of capital}}{1 + \text{inflation rate}} - 1$$

Key 47   Risk analysis in capital budgeting

OVERVIEW   *Risk analysis is important in making capital investment decisions because of the large amount of capital involved and the long-term nature of the investments. The higher the risk with a proposed project, the greater the rate of return that must be earned to compensate for that risk.*

Probability distributions: Expected value of a probability distribution may be computed. Before any capital budgeting method is applied, compute the expected cash inflows or, in some cases, the expected life of the asset.

Risk-adjusted discount rate: Adjust the *cost of capital* (or discount rate) upward as projects become riskier. The expected cash flows are discounted at the risk-adjusted discount rate; the usual capital budgeting criteria such as NPV or IRR are then applied.

Certainty equivalent: Financial decision makers determine the point at which they are indifferent to the choice between a certain sum of money and a risky sum of money.
- The certainty equivalent coefficient is multiplied by the original cash flow to obtain the equivalent certain cash flow.
- The risk-free rate of return is used as the discount rate under the NPV method and as the cutoff rate under the IRR method.

Simulation: A probability distribution is constructed for each of the important variables affecting the project's cash flows.

Sensitivity analysis: Forecasts of many calculated NPVs under various alternative functions are compared to see how sensitive NPV is to changing conditions.
- A certain variable or group of variables may drastically alter the NPV once their assumptions are changed or relaxed. This results in a much riskier asset than was originally forecast.

Decision trees: used to evaluate the risk of capital budgeting proposals. A decision tree is a graphical method of showing the sequence of possible outcomes. A capital budgeting tree shows the cash flows and NPV of a project under different circumstances.

Normal distribution and NPV analysis: With the assumption of independence of cash flows over time, the expected NPV is:

$$\text{Expected NPV} = \text{Expected PV} - I$$

$$= \sum_{t=1}^{n} \frac{\overline{A}_t}{(1 + r)^t} - I$$

- The standard deviation of NPVs is

$$\sigma = \sqrt{\sum_{t=1}^{n} \frac{\sigma^2_t}{(1 + r)^{2t}}}$$

- The expected value ($\overline{A}$) and the standard deviation (σ) give a considerable amount of information with which to assess the risk of an investment project.
- If the probability distribution is normal, some probability statement regarding the project's NPV can be made. For example, the probability of a project's providing NPV of less or greater than zero can be computed by standardizing the normal variate x as follows:

$$z = \frac{x - \text{NPV}}{\sigma}$$

where x = the outcome to be found
         NPV = the expected NPV
         z = the standardized normal variate

Theme 7 CAPITAL

*T*he cost of capital is the cost to the business of financing. An increase in the cost of capital to a company means it is viewed as an increasingly risky investment by the investing and credit community. As risk increases, interest rates and dividend yields increase. The break-even point is the amount of sales necessary to cover total costs; resulting in a zero profit. The cash break-even point—the volume of sales that will cover all cash expenses during a period—may also be determined. Operating leverage is the relationship of fixed cost to total cost; financial leverage is the extent to which debt exists in the capital structure. A major goal of the company is to maximize its market value through an optimal mix of long-term fund sources.

Key 48   Cost of capital

OVERVIEW   *Cost of capital is defined as the rate of return necessary to maintain the market value of the company (or price of the company's stock). Financial managers must know the cost of capital (the minimum required rate of return) in 1. making capital budgeting decisions, 2. helping to establish the optimal capital structure, and 3. making decisions about leasing, bond refunding, and managing working capital. The cost of capital is computed as a weighted average of the various capital components (items on the right side of the balance sheet, such as debt, preferred stock, common stock, and retained earnings).*

Determination of the company's cost of capital: Steps in measuring a firm's cost of capital are:
1. Compute the cost of each source of capital
2. Assign weights to each source
3. Compute the weighted average of the component costs

Computing individual costs of capital: each element of capital has a component cost that is identified by the following:
- k_i = before-tax cost of debt
- $k_d = k_i (1 - t)$ = after-tax cost of debt, where t = tax rate
- k_p = cost of preferred stock
- k_s = cost of retained earnings (or internal equity)
- k_e = cost of external equity, or cost of issuing new common stock
- k_o = firm's overall cost of capital, or a weighted average cost of capital

Cost of debt: yield to maturity (see Key 33). Since interest payments are tax deductible, the cost of debt must be stated on an after-tax basis as:

$$k_d = k_i (1 - t)$$

Cost of preferred stock: k_p is found by dividing the annual preferred stock dividend d_p by the net proceeds from the sale of the preferred stock p as follows:

$$k_p = \frac{d_p}{p}$$

- Since dividends are not tax deductible, there is no tax adjustment.

Cost of equity capital: See Key 49.

Cost of retained earnings: k_s is closely related to the cost of existing common stock, because the cost of equity obtained by retained earnings is the same as the rate of return investors require on the firm's common stock. Therefore,

$$k_e = k_s$$

Overall cost of capital: The overall cost of capital is the weighted average of the individual capital costs, with the weights being the proportions of each type of capital used. Let k_o be the overall cost of capital.

$$k_o = \sum \begin{array}{l} \text{\% of total capital structure} \\ \text{supplied by each type of} \\ \text{capital} \end{array} \times \begin{array}{l} \text{Cost of capital} \\ \text{for each source} \\ \text{of capital} \end{array}$$

$$= w_d \cdot k_d + w_p \cdot k_p + w_e \cdot k_e + w_s \cdot k_s$$

where w_d = % of total capital supplied by debt
w_p = % of total capital supplied by preferred stock
w_e = % of total capital supplied by external equity
w_s = % of total capital supplied by retained earnings (or internal equity)

Selection of weights: The weights can be:
- Historical (based on existing capital structure)
- Target (based on a "goal" capital structure)
- Marginal (based on proposed financing)

Level of financing and the marginal cost of capital (MCC): See Key 50.

Key 49 Computing the cost of equity capital

OVERVIEW *The cost of common stock, k_e, is generally viewed as the rate of return investors require on a firm's common stock.*

Methods of measuring the cost of equity capital: Two techniques for determining the cost of common stock are Gordon's Growth Model and the Capital Asset Pricing Model (CAPM).

Gordon's growth model: Solving for r results in the cost of common stock:

$$r = \frac{D_1}{P_o} + g \quad \text{or} \quad k_e = \frac{D_1}{P_o} + g$$

where P_o = value of common stock
D_1 = dividend to be received in 1 year
 r = investor's required rate of return
 g = rate of growth (assumed to be constant over time)
- The symbol r is changed to k_e to show that it is used to compute the cost of capital.
- The cost of new common stock is higher than the cost of existing common stock because of flotation costs (the costs of issuing a new security, including legal and printing fees).
- If f is flotation cost in percent, the denominator in the above equation becomes $P_o (1 - f)$.

Capital asset pricing model (CAPM): Cost of common stock is determined using the following steps:
1. Determine the risk-free rate, r_f (e.g., U.S. treasury bill rate).
2. Estimate the stock's beta coefficient, b (systematic risk).
3. Estimate the market rate of return, r_m (e.g., Dow Jones 30 Industrials).
5. Determine the required rate of return, k_e, on the company's stock:

$$k_e = r_f + b(r_m - r_f)$$

Key 50 Level of financing and the marginal cost of capital (MCC)

OVERVIEW *Since the amount of financing has an impact on a company's cost of capital, the expected return from an investment must be compared with the cost of financing the project. If the cost of capital rises as the level of financing increases, you should look at the marginal cost of capital, not the average cost of all funds financed. The investment should be limited to the amount at which IRR equals marginal cost of capital.*

The marginal cost of capital: Because external equity capital has a higher cost than retained earnings because of flotation costs, the weighted cost of capital increases for each dollar of new financing. Therefore, lower-cost capital sources are used first.

Calculation: The steps in calculating the company's marginal cost of capital are:
1. Determine the cost and the percentage of financing to be used for each source of capital (debt, preferred stock, common stock equity).
2. Compute the breakpoints on the MCC curve at which the weighted cost will increase. The formula for computing the breakpoints is:

$$\text{Break point} = \frac{\text{maximum amount of the lowest-cost source of capital}}{\text{percentage financing provided by the source}}$$

3. Calculate the weighted cost of capital over the range of total financing between breakpoints.
4. Construct a MCC schedule or graph that shows the weighted cost of capital for each level of total new financing.
5. This schedule is used in conjunction with the company's available investment opportunities schedule (IOS) to select the investments.

Key 51 Break-even analysis

OVERVIEW *Break-even analysis determines break-even sales, the level of sales at which total revenue equals total costs.*

Variable costs vs. fixed costs: To implement break-even analysis, the operating costs of a firm are separated into variable costs and fixed costs.

- *Variable costs:* costs that vary in total in direct proportions to volume. However, variable cost per unit remains the same. *Examples:* direct materials, direct labor, and sales commissions.
- *Fixed costs:* costs that remain constant regardless of activity level (assuming idle capacity). If volume increases, total fixed cost remains the same, but fixed cost per unit drops. *Examples:* depreciation, rent, and administrative salaries.

Break-even analysis: The break-even (BE) point is the quantity of output that results in earnings before interest and taxes (EBIT) equal to zero. The formula is:

$$BE = \frac{FC}{P - V}$$

where P = Unit selling price
   V = Unit variable cost
   FC = Fixed operating costs
(P − V) = Unit contribution margin

- To establish the break-even point in dollars, multiply the break-even units by the unit selling price.

Cash break-even point: See Key 52.

Determination of target income volume (TIV): The sales volume required to attain a particular income is computed as follows:

$$\text{Target sales volume} = \frac{FC + \text{target income}}{P - V}$$

Impact of taxes: If target income is given on an after-tax basis, the formula becomes:

$$\text{Target sales volume} = \frac{\text{Fixed costs} + \dfrac{\text{Target after-tax income}}{(1-\text{ tax rate})}}{\text{P-V}}$$

Margin of safety: a measure of difference between the actual level of sales and the break-even sales. It is the amount by which sales revenue may drop before losses begin and is expressed as a percentage of budgeted sales:

$$\text{Margin of safety} = \frac{\text{Budgeted sales} - \text{Break-even sales}}{\text{Budgeted sales}}$$

- The margin of safety is often used as a measure of risk. The larger the ratio, the safer the situation, because there is a lower risk of reaching the break-even point.

Break-even analysis assumptions: The break-even models assumes:
- The behavior of both sales revenue and expenses is linear throughout the entire relevant range of activity.
- There is only one product or a constant sales mix.
- Volume is the only factor affecting variable costs.
- Inventories do not change significantly from period to period.

Key 52 Cash break-even point

OVERVIEW *If a firm has a minimum of available cash or if the opportunity cost of holding excess cash is high, management may want to know the volume of sales necessary to cover all cash expenses during a period. This volume is known as the cash break-even point.*

Cash break-even (CBE) sales: unit or dollar sales volume at which operating cash receipts equal operating cash disbursements.
- Not all fixed operating costs involve cash payments. For example, depreciation expense and amortization are noncash charges.
- To find the cash break-even point, subtract noncash charges from total fixed operating costs.
- The cash break-even point is lower than the usual break-even point.
- The formula is:

$$CBE = \frac{FC - NC}{P - V}$$

where P = selling price per unit, V = unit variable cost, FC = fixed operating costs, and NC = noncash expenses included in fixed costs.

KEY EXAMPLE

If the selling price is $25, the variable cost is $15 per unit, and total fixed cost is $50,000, including depreciation of $2,000, the cash break-even point is:

$$CBE = \frac{\$50,000 - \$2,000}{\$25 - \$15} = 4,800 \text{ units}$$

Key 53 Leverage

OVERVIEW *Leverage is that portion of fixed costs that represents risk to the firm. Operating leverage, a measure of operating risk, refers to the fixed operating costs found in the firm's income statement. Financial leverage, a measure of financial risk, refers to the practice of financing a portion of the firm's assets through debts bearing fixed financing charges in hopes of increasing the return to the common stockholders. The higher the financial leverage, the higher the financial risk and the higher the cost of capital.*

Degrees of operating, financial, and total leverage: Let us define:
- X = Sales volume in units
- P = Selling price per unit
- V = Unit variable cost
- FC = Fixed operating costs
- I = Fixed financial costs (primarily interest costs arising from debt financing that must be paid regardless of the level of sales or profit.)

Operating leverage: See Key 54.

Financial leverage: See Key 55.

Total leverage: Total leverage is measured by determining how EPS is affected by a change in sales.

KEY EQUATION

Total leverage at a given level of sales (X) equals:

$$\frac{\text{Percentage in change in EPS}}{\text{Percentage in change in sales}} = \text{operating leverage} \times \text{financial leverage}$$

$$= \frac{(P - V)X}{(P - V)X - FC} \cdot \frac{(P - V)X - FC}{(P - V)X - FC - I}$$

$$= \frac{(P - V)X}{(P - V)X - FC - I}$$

Key 54 Operating leverage

OVERVIEW *Operating leverage, a measure of operating risk, refers to the fixed operating costs found in the firm's income statement.*

Degree of operating leverage (DOL): measures the sensitivity of a firm's operating income (or EBIT) to a change in sales.
- The use of operating leverage increases the potential return but also increases potential operating risk.
- Operating leverage at a given level of sales (X) equals:

$$\frac{\text{Percentage change in EBIT}}{\text{Percentage change in sales}} = \frac{(P - V)X}{(P - V)X - FC}$$

where EBIT = earnings before interest and taxes
$$= (P - V)X - FC$$

- Operating leverage tells how many times earnings go up if sales increase by 1 percent.
- Another measure of operating leverage (risk) is the ratio of fixed costs to total costs. High fixed costs indicate risks because they cannot be slashed in the short run to meet declining demand for the product or service.

Operating leverage and break-even point: The break-even point is closely allied to operating leverage because a lower break-even point means lower operating risk.

Key 55 Financial leverage

OVERVIEW *Financial leverage, also called trading on equity, is that portion of a firm's assets that are financed with debt instead of equity. It involves contractual interest and principal payments. Trading profitably on equity, also known as positive (favorable) financial leverage, means that the borrowed funds generate a higher rate of return than the interest rate paid for the use of the funds. The excess accrues to the benefit of the owners because it magnifies, or increases, their earnings.*

Financial leverage: a measure of financial risk arising from fixed financial costs.
- One way to measure financial leverage is to determine how earnings per share (EPS) are affected by a change in EBIT (or operating income).
- Financial leverage at a given level of sales (X) equals:

$$\frac{\text{Percentage in change in EPS}}{\text{Percentage in change in EBIT}} = \frac{\text{EBIT}}{\text{EBIT} - \text{I}} = \frac{(P - V)X - FC}{(P - V)X - FC - I}$$

Financial ratios: Financial leverage is also measured by various financial ratios, such as the debt-equity ratio and the times-interest-earned ratio. See Key 12.

Adverse effects of excessive financial leverage: If a company's debt position is excessive, there will be adverse effects including:
- Bankruptcy resulting from an inability to meet principal or interest payments
- An increase in the overall cost of capital
- An inability to obtain financing at reasonable rates and terms

Key 56   Theory of capital structure

OVERVIEW   *The theory of capital structure is closely related to the company's cost of capital. Capital structure is the mix of the long-term sources of funds used by the company. The primary objective of capital structure decisions is to maximize the market value of the company through an appropriate mix of long-term sources of funds. This mix, called the optimal capital structure, minimizes the overall cost of capital; however, there is disagreement about whether an optimal capital structure actually exists.*

Approaches to the theory of capital structure: 1. net operating income, 2. net income, 3. traditional, and 4. Miller-Modigliani. All four of these approaches use the following simplifying assumptions:

- No income taxes are included
- The company's dividend payout is 100%
- No transaction costs are incurred
- The company has constant earnings before interest and taxes (EBIT).
- There is a constant operating risk.

Rates: Given these assumptions, the company is concerned with the following three rates:

1.
$$k_i = \frac{I}{B}$$

where k_i = cost or yield on the firm's debt (assuming a perpetuity)
   I = annual interest charges
   B = market value of debt outstanding

2.
$$k_e = \frac{EAC}{S}$$

where k_e = the firm's required rate of return on equity or cost of common equity (assuming no earnings growth and a 100% dividend payout ratio)
   EAC = earnings available to common stockholders
   S = market value of stock outstanding

$$3. \qquad k_o = \frac{EBIT}{V}$$

where k_o = the firm's overall cost of capital
        EBIT = earnings before interest and taxes
           V = the market value of the firm (B + S)

Effect of leverage: In each of the four approaches to determining capital structure, the concern is with what happens to k_i, k_e, and k_o when the degree of leverage, as denoted by the debt-equity (B/S) ratio, increases.

The net operating income (NOI) approach: suggests that there is no one optimal capital structure and that the firm's overall cost of capital, k_o, and the value of the firm's market value of debt and stock outstanding, V, are both independent of the degree to which the company uses leverage.

The net income (NI) approach: assumes that k_i and k_e remain unchanged as the debt-equity ratio increases and both the overall cost of capital, k_o, and the market value of the firm, V, are affected by the firm's use of leverage.
- The firm is able to increase its value, V, and lower its cost of capital, k_o, as it increases the degree of leverage.

Traditional approach: assumes that there is an optimal capital structure and that the firm can increase its value through leverage. This moderate view of the relationship between leverage and valuation encompasses all the ground between the NOI approach and the NI approach.

Miller-Modigliana (MM) position: MM asserts that :
- The market value of the firm and its cost of capital are independent of its capital structure.
- k_e increases to offset exactly the use of cheaper debt money.
- The cutoff rate for capital budgeting decisions is completely independent of the way in which an investment is financed.

Factors affecting capital structure: Some factors impacting upon a company's capital structure are: 1. growth rate and stability of future sales, 2. industry competition, 3. asset makeup, and 4. risk preferences.

The Black-Scholes option pricing model: used to determine the equilibrium value of an option. Provides insight into the valuation of debt relative to equity.

KEY FORMULA

Present value of call option = $PN(d_1) - EXe^{-r_f t}N(d_2)$

where P = price of stock now

   N(d) = cumulative normal probability density function

    EX = exercise price of option

     t = time to exercise date

    r_f = (continuously compounded) risk-free rate of interest

    e = 2.71828

$$d_1 = \frac{\log (P/EX) + r_f t + \sigma^2 t/2}{\sigma \cdot \sqrt{t}}$$

$$d_1 = \frac{\log (P/EX) + r_f t + \sigma^2 t/2}{\sigma \cdot \sqrt{t}}$$

σ^2 = variance per period of (continuously compounded) rate of return on the stock

The formula, while somewhat imposing, actually uses readily available input data, with the exception of σ, or volatility. P, EX, r_f, and t are easily obtained.

The implication of the option model: The value of the option increases with the level of stock price relative to the exercise price (P/EX), the time to expiration times the interest rate ($r_f t$), and the time to expiration times the stock's variability ($\sigma^2 \cdot t$).

- The option price is always less than the stock price.
- The optional price never falls below the payoff to immediate exercise (P − EX or zero, whichever is larger).
- If the stock is worthless, the option is worthless.
- As the stock price becomes very large, the option price approaches the stock price less the present value of the exercise price.

Key 57 EBIT-EPS approach to capital structure

OVERVIEW *Financial managers use the EBIT-EPS approach to capital structure to evaluate alternative financing plans. It helps achieve an optimal capital structure, resulting in the lowest overall cost of capital.*

Use of financial leverage: Financial leverage affects earnings in two ways:
- Risk to EPS rises because of the use of fixed financial obligations.
- The level of EPS changes at a given EBIT in association with a specific capital structure.
- The first effect is measured by the degree of financial leverage.
- The second effect is analyzed by means of EBIT-EPS analysis. The financial manager evaluates alternative financing plans by investigating their effect on EPS over a range of EBIT levels.

EPS-EBIT analysis: Primary objective is to determine the EBIT break-even or indifference points for various alternative financing plans.

KEY EQUATION

The indifference points between any two methods of financing can be determined by solving for EBIT in the following equality:

$$\frac{(EBIT - I)(1 - t) - PD}{S_1} = \frac{(EBIT - I)(1 - t) - PD}{S_2}$$

where t = tax rate
PD = preferred stock dividends
S_1 and S_2 = number of shares of common stock outstanding after financing for plan 1 and plan 2, respectively.

Theme 8 DIVIDENDS AND STOCK SPLITS

*C*ash and stock represent the major types of dividends a company may issue to its stockholders. Cash dividends may be stated on a per-share basis or on a percentage-of-par-value basis. Generally, stockholders look favorably upon a company that issues dividends. However, a growth company typically retains most of its earnings for expansion. A stock split occurs when a company changes the par value per share by issuing more shares; a 2-for-1 split reduces the par value per share by one-half.

INDIVIDUAL KEYS IN THIS THEME

Key 58   Cash dividends

OVERVIEW   *A cash dividend is typically expressed in dollars-and-cents per share based on outstanding shares. However, the dividend on preferred stock is often expressed as a percentage of par value.*

Declaration date: date the board of directors declares the dividend, making it a legal liability of the company.

Date of record: date on which the stockholder has a right to receive the dividend.

Ex-dividend date: date on which the right to the dividend leaves the shares. The right to a dividend stays with the stock until 4 days before the date of record. The market price of the stock reflects the fact that it has gone ex-dividend and will decrease by approximately the amount of the dividend.

Date of payment: date on which the company distributes dividend checks to its stockholders.

Computations:
- If a cash dividend per share is declared, the dividend equals the dividends per share times the outstanding shares. *Example:* A cash dividend per share of $1.20 on 10,000 outstanding shares results in a dividend of $12,000 ($1.20 × 10,000).
- If a percentage cash dividend is declared, the dividend equals the percentage times the total par value of the outstanding shares. *Example:* A company has 30,000 shares of $10 par value, 8% preferred stock outstanding. The dividend equals $24,000 (30,000 × $10 × 8%).

Dividend reinvestment plan: A company may give its stockholders the option of automatically investing their dividends in corporate shares instead of receiving cash.

Key 59   Stock dividends and stock splits

OVERVIEW   *A* stock dividend *is the issuance of additional shares of stock to stockholders.* A stock split *is the issuance of a significant amount of additional shares, reducing the par value per share of the stock on a proportional basis.*

Characteristics of a stock dividend: A stock dividend is a pro rata distribution of additional shares of a corporation's own stock to its stockholders. While a stock dividend increases the number of shares held, the proportion of the company each stockholder owns remains the same.
- A stock dividend may be declared when the cash position of the company is deficient and/or when the company wants to prompt more trading of its stock by reducing its market price.

Characteristics of a stock split: A stock split increases a company's outstanding shares without changing the total par value of the stock; the par value per share is proportionately reduced. *Example:* If a company with 10,000 shares of $10 par value stock issues a 2-for-1 stock split, there will then be 20,000 shares at a $5 par value. The total par value will remain at $100,000.
- After a stock split, theoretically the market price per share of the stock should drop proportionately. *Example:* After a 4-for-1 stock split, the market price per share should drop to one-fourth of what it was before the split.
- A stock split may be prompted by a desire to reduce the market price per share to make it easier for small investors to purchase shares.

Similarities between a stock dividend and stock split: 1. outstanding shares increase, 2. total stockholders' equity remains the same, and 3. no cash is paid.

Key 60 Dividend policy

OVERVIEW *Dividends should fulfill the objectives of both the stockholders and company.*

Policies: The more stable a company's earnings, the more regular its issuance of dividends. However, if cash flow and investment requirements are volatile, the company should avoid establishing a high regular dividend. If dividends are increased, they should continue at the higher rate since stockholders will expect them to do so.

Reasons dividend policy is important:
- Affects investor attitudes. Stockholders usually look negatively on a company that cuts its dividends.
- Impacts the company's financing program and capital budget.
- Affects the company's cash position. A company with liquidity problems may have to restrict or cease dividend payments.

Factors that influence dividend policy:
- *Net income:* A higher net income allows for more dividends.
- *Earnings stability:* A stable earnings usually result in more dividends.
- *Growth rate:* A rapidly growing company often restricts dividends in order to retain funds in the business to promote further growth.
- *Debt position:* A highly leveraged business is more likely to retain earnings to satisfy principal and interest payments on debt.
- *Loan restrictions:* Dividends may be restricted in accordance with a loan agreement.
- *Internal financing:* A company that wants to finance its operations internally will retain greater earnings. Internal financing is the least costly financing source.
- *Ability to finance externally:* A company with easy access to the capital markets can afford a higher dividend payout.
- *Maturity and size:* A mature, large company has easier access to outside financing and has less need to retain profits.
- *Taxes:* Tax penalties may be assessed for excess accumulated retained earnings.

Types of dividend policies:
- *Stable dividends-per-share policy:* This policy is typically looked on favorably by investors. Dividend stability implies a low-risk company. Some financial institutions and private investors invest only in companies with stable dividends, and individuals relying on a fixed income also favor stable dividends.

- *Constant dividend-payout-ratio (dividends per share/earnings per share) policy:* A constant percentage of earnings is paid out in dividends. Since net income varies, the dividends also vary. Most stockholders do not like fluctuation in dividends.
- *Compromise policy:* A compromise between policies 1 and 2 may be suitable for a company. *Example:* A company pays a low dollar amount per share plus a percentage increment in good years. The increment should not be paid regularly because stockholders come to expect it. This policy may be advisable when profitability shows wide variation.
- *Residual-dividend policy:* If a firm's investment opportunities are unstable, the company may opt for a fluctuating dividend policy in which the amount of earnings retained depends on the availability of investment opportunities in a given year.

Theoretical position: Theoretically a company should retain earnings rather than distribute them when the corporate return exceeds the return investors can obtain on their money elsewhere.
- If the company's return on profits exceeds the cost of capital, market price of stock will rise. However, practically speaking, investors will expect to receive dividends.

Theme 9 SHORT-TERM FINANCING

A company may use short-term funds, those payable within one year, for financing. Balances owed to suppliers are typically cost-free because they carry no interest. Commercial paper is unsecured short-term debt offered at a low interest rate by larger, financially healthy companies. Bank loans usually bear interest rates at or above the prime interest rate, with the prime rate offered to the most financially strong borrowers. When a company has difficulty obtaining a loan from a bank, it may go to commercial finance companies, which typically charge higher interest rates. Accounts receivable and inventory may serve as collateral for a loan or advance.

INDIVIDUAL KEYS IN THIS THEME	
61	Financing strategy
62	Trade credit
63	Short-term bank loans
64	Other sources of financing
65	Acounts receivable financing
66	Inventory financing

Key 61 Financing strategy

OVERVIEW *The financial manager is concerned about selecting the best possible source of financing based on the company's particular situation.*

Considerations in formulating a financing strategy:
- The cost and risk associated with alternative financing instruments
- The tax rate. Since interest is tax-deductible, a higher tax rate makes debt more attractive.
- The maturity dates of debt securities. If liquidity is a problem, the maturity dates should be extended.
- The present ratio of debt to equity. If debt is excessive, equity financing may be a better choice.
- The adequacy of current lines of credit to meet current and future needs
- The inflation rate. In an inflationary economy, repayment of debt is made in cheaper dollars.
- The company's earning power and liquidity. High earnings and liquidity make it easier to repay debt obligations.
- The amount, nature, and stability of internally-generated funds
- The restrictions in existing loan agreements on incurring additional debt
- The future trend in capital market conditions
- The type and amount of collateral required by long-term creditors
- The ability to modify the financing strategy to adjust to changing economic conditions

Short-term vs. long-term financing: Short-term financing typically involves a lower cost than long-term financing because long-term financing involves more uncertainty. Short-term financing involves greater liquidity risk because payment is due within one year.
- Long-term financing is more suitable if a company has current financial problems but expects things to improve in the future.

Key 62 Trade credit

OVERVIEW *Trade credit (accounts payable) are balances owed to suppliers. It is a short-term financing source.*

Characteristics:
- A spontaneous source of financing because it arises from normal business operations
- Least expensive form of financing inventory
- Carries either no interest or a minimal amount

Advantages:
- Readily available since suppliers want business
- Collateral is not required
- Convenient
- Trade creditors usually lenient if corporate financial problems occur
- Accounts payable may be stretched out within reason

Opportunity cost of foregoing a cash discount: net revenue lost by not taking advantage of a discount offered by a trade creditor.

KEY FORMULA

The formula used to compute the opportunity cost in percentage, on an annual basis, of not taking a discount is:

$$\text{Opportunity cost} = \frac{\text{Discount foregone}}{\text{Proceeds use of}} \times \frac{360}{N}$$

where N = the number of days payment can be delayed by foregoing the discount
= days credit is outstanding less discount period

Key 63 Short-term bank loans

OVERVIEW *A company with a satisfactory financial position may borrow money from the bank. When a bank loan is taken, the debtor typically signs a note, a written promise to repay the loan at the due date. A note payable may be paid at maturity or in installments. A short-term bank loan is payable within one year or less.*

Interest:
- The prime interest rate is the lowest interest rate applied to bank loans. Banks charge only their most creditworthy clients the prime rate.
- Interest on a bank loan equals: interest rate × principal × time. *Example:* = The interest on a $10,000, 12% six-month loan is: 12% × $10,000 × 6/12 = $600
- Interest on a loan may be paid either at maturity (ordinary interest) or in advance (discounting the loan).
- When interest is paid in advance, the proceeds from the loan are reduced and the effective (true) interest cost is increased.

$$\text{Proceeds} = \text{Principal} - \text{Interest}$$

- Effective interest rate equals interest divided by proceeds. *Example:* The effective interest rate on a $50,000, 14%, one-year bank loan on a discount basis equals:

$$\frac{\text{Interest}}{\text{Proceeds}} = \frac{\$7,000}{\$50,000 - \$7,000} = \frac{\$7,000}{\$43,000} = 16.3\%$$

- When a loan has a compensating balance requirement (a deposit maintained with the bank that does not earn interest), the proceeds received are decreased by the amount of the compensating balance. The compensating balance increases the effective interest rate.

$$\text{Adjusted proceeds} =$$
$$\text{principal} - \text{interest} - \text{compensating balance}$$

- Effective interest rate equals interest divided by adjusted proceeds. *Example:* A $60,000, 19%, one-year bank loan on a discount basis is taken. The compensating balance is 15%. The effective interest rate equals:

$$\frac{\text{Interest}}{\text{Proceeds}} = \frac{\$11,400}{(\$60,000 - \$11,400 - \$9,000)} = \frac{\$11,400}{\$39,600} = 28.8\%$$

Unsecured loan: A loan without a collateral requirement; usually given to companies with excellent credit ratings to finance projects that have quick cash flows. *Disadvantages*: 1. usually has a higher interest rate than a secured loan; and 2. requires payment in a lump sum.

Secured loan: a collateral-backed loan, usually required for borrowers with questionable credit ratings.

Line of credit: an agreement from a bank to lend money to the borrower on a recurring basis up to a specified amount. Credit lines are usually established for a one-year period and may be renewed annually.
- *Advantages:* 1. provide easy and immediate access to funds during tight money markets, and 2. enable you to borrow only as much as necessary and to repay immediately when cash is available.
- *Disadvantages*: 1. require commitment fee on the unused credit line, 2. may require compensating balance on the unused portion, 3. require collateral, and 4. may impose restrictions on the company (e.g., minimum working capital).

Installment loan: a loan requiring monthly payments. *Advantage*: may be tailored to satisfy a company's seasonal financing needs.

Key 64 Other sources of financing

OVERVIEW *Financing can be arranged through banker's acceptances, commercial paper, or from finance companies.*

Banker's acceptances. A banker's acceptance is a draft, drawn by an individual and accepted by a bank, that orders payment to a third party at a later date.
- The draft's creditworthiness is high since it is backed by the bank.
- A draft is a debt instrument created by the creditor out of a self-liquidating business transaction.
- It is often used to finance shipment and handling of domestic and foreign merchandise.
- It is a marketable instrument.
- Acceptances are classed as short-term financing because the maturity date is usually under 180 days.

Commercial paper: unsecured, short-term debt issued on a discount basis by financially strong companies with high credit ratings.
- Interest rate below prime
- No collateral required
- Short-term maturity, usually under 270 days
- Issued at discount. The interest is immediately deducted by the creditor, but the debtor pays the full face value.
- Issued through a dealer or directly by an institutional investor
- Rated by Standard and Poor's and by Moody's
- Issued only by large, financially sound companies

Commercial finance companies: When short-term credit cannot be obtained from the bank, a company may go to a commercial finance company.
- A finance company loan has a higher interest rate than a bank loan.
- The loan is typically secured by collateral—including inventory, accounts receivable, and fixed assets—whose value exceeds the balance of the loan.
- The finance company may also finance installment purchases of industrial equipment.

Key 65   Accounts receivable financing

OVERVIEW   *Receivable financing uses short-term financing backed by receivables. Accounts receivable financing may be a factoring or an assignment arrangement.*

Characteristics: The financing of accounts receivable is facilitated if customers are financially strong, sales returns are minimal, and title to the goods is received by the buyer at shipment.

Factoring: outright sale of accounts receivable to a third party *without recourse*; the purchaser assumes all credit and collection risks.
- The proceeds received by the selling company equal the face value of the receivables less the commission charge, usually 2 to 5% above the prime interest rate.
- The cost of factoring is the factor's commission for credit investigation, interest on the unpaid balance of advanced funds, and a discount from the face value of the receivables.
- Billing and collection is done by the factor.

Advantages: 1. seller receives immediate cash, 2. overhead is reduced because credit investigation is no longer needed, 3. seller can obtain advances as needed on a seasonal basis, and 4. seller can receive financial advice.

Disadvantages: 1. high cost, 2. possible negative customer reaction, and 3. pressure applied by factors to customers who are past due may arouse antagonism.

Assignment: assigning accounts receivable with *recourse;* if the customer does not pay, the company (borrower) has to pay. The accounts receivable act as collateral; and new receivables substitute for receivables collected.
- There is no transfer of ownership of accounts receivable.
- The finance company usually advances between 50 and 85% of the face value of the receivables in cash.
- The borrower incurs a service charge, interest on the advance, and bad debt losses.
- Customer remissions continue to be made to the company.

Advantages: 1. cash immediately available, 2. cash advances received on a seasonal basis, and 3. negative customer reaction avoided.

Disadvantages: 1. high cost, 2. continued credit investment function, and 3. significant credit risks.

Key 66   Inventory financing

OVERVIEW   *Inventory financing is the use of inventory as collateral for a loan. It typically occurs when a company has fully exhausted its borrowing capacity on receivables.*

Type of inventory: Inventory financing requires the existence of marketable, nonperishable, standardized goods with fast turnover. Inventory should preferably be stable in price; expenses associated with its sale should be minimal.

Financing: the advance is usually higher for readily marketable inventory. Generally, 75% of the value of raw materials and finished goods can be financed. The interest rate is approximately 3 to 5 points over the prime interest rate.

Ways to finance inventory:
- *Floating (blanket) lien:* uses entire inventory as the creditor's security.
- *Warehouse receipt:* provides the lender an interest in the borrower's inventory stored at a public warehouse. The fixed cost of this arrangement is high. In a field warehouse arrangement, the warehouser sets up a secured area directly at the debtor's location.
- *Trust receipt:* gives the creditor title to the goods but releases them to the borrower to sell on the creditor's behalf. As goods are sold, the borrower pays the lender. An example is automobile dealer financing.
- *A collateral certificate:* may be issued by a third party to the lender guaranteeing the existence of pledged inventory.

Disadvantages of inventory financing:
- High interest rate.
- Restrictions placed on the inventory.

Theme 10   TERM LOANS AND
LEASING

*I*ntermediate-term loans, while carrying an interest rate typically higher than that on a short-term loan, have less liquidity risk. Loan payments include principal and interest. However, restrictive provisions often exist in loan agreements. A small business having difficulty obtaining a loan from a bank may contact the Small Business Administration. Equipment may serve as collateral for an advance or loan; a company may also rent real or personal property by making periodic payments. Although the total cost of leasing is typically higher than the cost of buying the item, leasing has many advantages, including the absence of a substantial initial payment, the avoidance of obsolescence risk, and existence of fewer financing restrictions than with a loan.

Key 67 Intermediate-term bank loans

OVERVIEW *Intermediate-term bank loans have a maturity of more than one year. Such loans are used when short-term unsecured loans are not appropriate, such as for the acquisition of a long-term asset.*

Interest: The interest rate on an intermediate-term loan is usually higher than that on a short-term loan because of the longer maturity date.
- The interest rate may be either fixed or variable (depending on some factor) over the term of the loan.
- The interest rate depends on the financial strength of the borrower and the amount of the loan.

Payment schedule: The loan is usually payable in periodic equal installments except for the last payment, which may be higher (so-called balloon payment).
- The schedule of loan payments should be based on the borrower's cash flow position.
- The amortization payment (see Key 36) equals:

$$\frac{\text{Amount of loan}}{\text{Present value of annuity of \$1 (PVAIF)}}$$

Amortization: Each loan payment contains both principal on the loan and interest. Over time, more of the loan payment is used to reduce the principal as the interest on the balance of the loan keeps dropping. A loan amortization schedule shows the breakdown of the interest and the repayment of principal. *Example:* A \$14,938.80 loan, payable in 20 equal year-end annual installments of \$2,000 each, is taken out. The interest rate is 12%. The payment schedule for the first two years follows:

Year	Payment	Interest (12% × Balance)	Principal	Balance
0				\$14,938.80
1	\$2,000	\$1,792.66	\$207.34	14,731.46
2	2,000	1,767.78	232.22	14,499.24

Revolving credit: The notes documenting a revolving credit (loan period in excess of one year) are short-term, typically 90 days. Such credit is often used for seasonal financing. *Advantages:* 1. is flexible and readily available, and 2. has fewer financing restrictions than a line of credit. *Disadvantage:* slightly higher interest rate than a line of credit.

- Within the time period of the revolving credit agreement, the company may renew a loan or engage in additional financing up to a specified maximum amount.

Advantages of intermediate-term loans: 1. avoids possible nonrenewal of a short-term loan, 2. offers flexible terms, 3. provides confidentiality for financial information, 4. is obtained faster than proceeds from a public offering, and 5. carries no flotation costs.

Disadvantages of intermediate-term loans: 1. require collateral, 2. have restrictive covenants, 3. require submission of periodic financial statements and reports to the bank; and 4. may require "kickers" or "sweeteners," such as stock warrants or a share of the profits, for the bank.

Equipment financing: An intermediate-term loan may be secured by a company's equipment. Equipment financing may be obtained from banks, finance companies, or manufacturers of equipment.
- An advance is made against the market value of the equipment; the more marketable the equipment is, the higher the advance will be.
- The cost of selling the equipment, if need be, is a consideration to the creditor.
- The repayment schedule is designed so that the market value of the equipment at a given time exceeds the unpaid balance of the loan.

Key 68 Small Business Administration

OVERVIEW *A small business may obtain financing from the U.S. Small Business Administration (SBA). Size standards have been established by type of business and are subject to change.*

Eligibility: The small business must have first applied to private sources (e.g., banks) and have been refused a loan on reasonable terms. To obtain an SBA loan, you may have to put up collateral. The SBA provides eligibility and financial counseling.

SBA business loans:
- Loans made by a private lender and guaranteed by the SBA
- Loans made directly by the SBA
- Both are subject to a maximum dollar amount and maturity
- The interest rate on an SBA loan may be slightly less than the going interest rate in the money market

SBA economic opportunity loans: have the following characteristics:
- Restricted to those of low income or disadvantaged
- Collateral required
- Subject to a dollar and maturity ceiling

Key 69   Leasing

OVERVIEW   *A lease is a long-term rental of real or personal property by the lessee.*

Lease contract: A lease agreement contains the following provisions: 1. lease term, 2. renewal option, 3. rental rate, 4. cancellation provision, 5. value of leased item, 6. location where leased item may be used, and 7. maintenance and insurance responsibility.

Types of leases:
- *Operating (service) lease:* involves both financing and maintenance services. The lessor may be the manufacturer of the asset or a leasing company. The lease payments are generally not sufficient to recover the full cost of the property. A cancellation clause that may be exercised by the lessee before the expiration date of the agreement usually exists.
- *Financial lease:* does not typically provide for maintenance services and is noncancellable. Rental payments equal the full price of the leased property.
- *Sale and leaseback:* agreement in which a company sells an asset to another company (usually a financial institution) and then leases it back. This provides needed cash to the company from sale while allowing it to continue to use the property.
- *Leveraged lease:* involves a third party. A lessor borrows money from the lender in order to buy the asset, which is then leased to the lessee.

Advantages of leasing: 1. does not require immediate cash payment, 2. may contain a bargain purchase option, 3. may allow the lessee in effect to depreciate the land leased, 4. may enable the lessee to avoid the obsolescence risk, 5. makes available the lessor's expert service, 6. has fewer financing restrictions than a loan taken out to buy the property, 7. has a limit of 3 years of lease payments or claims by the lessor in the event of the lessee's bankruptcy or reorganization, and 8. does not require the obligation for future rental payment to be recognized on the balance sheet.

Disadvantages of leasing: 1. in the long run, has a higher cost than buying the property, 2. may call for a higher interest rate than a loan, 3. may leave the lessee with obsolete or inefficient property, 4. requires the lessee to obtain the owner's consent for improvements to the leased property, and 5. may require the lessee to sign a new lease or buy the property at higher current prices at the end of the lease.

Theme 11 LONG-TERM DEBT

*L*ong-term debt includes mortgages and bonds payable. Mortgages are collateralized by real property and require periodic loan payments. A bond payable is a certificate obligating the company to pay periodic interest charges and the face value of the debt at maturity. The terms of the bond issue are specified in the indenture. Bonds may be unsecured or secured. A company may choose to retire its bonds early, such as when interest rates have dropped.

INDIVIDUAL KEYS IN THIS THEME

70   Long-term debt financing

71   Bond refunding

Key 70 Long-term debt financing

OVERVIEW *The characteristics, advantages, and disadvantages of long-term debt should be considered in financing a company.*

Mortgages: notes payable collateralized by real assets and requiring periodic payments consisting of interest and principal.
- The types of mortgages are: 1. *senior mortgage* (first claim on assets and earnings), and 2. *junior mortgage* (subordinate lien).
- Mortgage provisions include: 1. *closed-end,* in which the company cannot issue additional debt of the same priority against the same property, and 2. *open-end,* in which the company can issue additional first-mortgage bonds against the property.

Advantages of mortgages: lower interest rates, extended maturity, and fewer financing restrictions than other forms of long-term debt.

Bonds payable: certificates documenting the loan of a specific sum of money that will be repaid at a later date.
- The *indenture* is a written agreement describing the features of the bond issue. If a provision is violated, the bonds are in default.
- Bonds are issued in $1,000 denominations and typically have maturities of 10 to 30 years.
- The price of a bond depends on many factors, including interest rate, maturity date, and collateral.
- Interest equals nominal (coupon) interest rate × face value of bond × fraction of year outstanding. (See Key 33.)

Types of bonds:
- *Debentures:* unsecured debt that can be issued only by large, financially sound companies with superior credit ratings.
- *Subordinated debentures:* unsecured debt in which the claims of bondholders are subordinated to senior creditors.
- *Mortgage bonds:* bonds secured by real assets.
- *Collateral trust bonds:* bonds secured by the issuer's security investments (stocks or bonds).
- *Convertible bonds:* bonds that may be converted to stock at a future date.
- *Income bonds:* bonds that pay interest only if the issuer has earnings.
- *Guaranteed bonds:* bonds whose payment is guaranteed by a third party.
- *Serial bonds:* bonds that mature in installments.

- *Zero-coupon bonds:* bonds having a zero coupon rate. The issuer receives the proceeds at the time of issuance but pays the bonds back at a much higher face value on the maturity date.
- *Deep discount bonds:* bonds issued with very low coupons or at a price far below par value.

Advantages of issuing long-term debt: 1. interest is tax-deductible, while dividends are not, 2. bondholders do not participate in superior earnings of the company, 3. common stockholders' interest and voting rights are not diluted, and 4. in an inflationary economy, the debt is repaid in cheaper dollars.

Disadvantages of issuing long-term debt: 1. interest must be paid irrespective of corporate earnings, 2. the principal on the debt must be repaid at the maturity date, 3. a higher debt position implies greater risk and a higher cost of capital, and 4. restrictive provisions may be placed on the company.

Suitability of debt financing: Debt financing is more appropriate when: 1. revenue and earnings are stable, 2. profit margin is satisfactory, 3. liquidity and cash flow are good, 4. debt/equity ratio is low, 5. stock prices are depressed, 6. inflation is expected, and 7. indenture restrictions are not burdensome.
- A company with financial problems may decide to refinance short-term debt on a long-term basis, perhaps by extending the maturity dates of loans.

Key 71   Bond refunding

OVERVIEW   *Bonds may be refunded by the company prior to maturity either by the issuance of a serial bond or by exercising a call privilege on a straight bond. The issuance of serial bonds allows the company to refund the debt over the life of the issue.*

Call feature: When interest rates are expected to decline, a call provision in the bond issue that enables the company to buy back the high-interest bond and issue a low-interest one is recommended. The timing of the refunding depends on expected future interest rates.
- A call price is usually established in excess of the face value of the bond. The resulting call premium equals the difference between the call price and the maturity value.
- The call premium is generally equal to one year's interest if the bond is called in the first year; it declines at a constant rate each year thereafter.

Bond refunding decision: The desirability of refunding a bond requires *net present value analysis,* which involves the following steps:
- Step 1. Calculate the initial outlay.
- Step 2. Calculate the annual cash benefit of eliminating the old bonds through refunding.
- Step 3. Calculate the annual cash outflow of issuing the new bonds.
- Step 4. Calculate the annual net cash benefits (that is, difference between Step 2 and Step 3) from the refunding decision.
- Step 5. Calculate the present value of the annual net cash benefits.
- Step 6. Calculate the refunding decision's net present value (that is, difference between Step 5 and Step 1).

Theme 12 STOCK, CONVERTIBLES, AND WARRANTS

*I*nvestment bankers act as the intermediary between companies issuing securities and investors buying them. Two types of stock may be issued to stockholders: preferred stock and common stock. Preferred stock has priority over common stock in the event of liquidation and the distribution of earnings; however, common stock benefits most if the company is successful. Convertible preferred stock or convertible bonds may be exchanged by the holder for common stock at a later date. A stock warrant gives the holder the option to purchase a specified number of shares of stock at a given price by a particular date.

INDIVIDUAL KEYS IN THIS THEME

72	Investment banking
73	Public versus private placement of securities
74	Stockholders
75	Preferred stock
76	Common stock
77	Stock rights
78	Stock repurchases
79	Margin trading
80	Short selling
81	Governmental regulation
82	Efficient market theory
83	Convertible securities
84	Stock warrants

Key 72   Investment banking

OVERVIEW   *Investment banking concerns the public issuance of a security. The investment banker is the middleman between the issuing company and the investor.*

Functions of investment banking:
- *Underwriting:* buying a security issue, paying the issuer, and marketing the security.
- *Distributing:* marketing the security issue.
- *Providing advice:* advising the company on the terms and features of the issue as well as on the best ways to raise funds.
- *Providing funds:* furnishing funds to the issuing company during the distribution period.

Syndicate: group of investment bankers for a new, large, and/or risky issue.
- The investment banker who manages the syndicate and underbanker is limited to the terms of participation.
- In an *undivided account,* each member is liable for unsold securities up to the amount of its percentage participation regardless of the number of securities that investment banker has sold. The undivided type is the more common one.

Best efforts: The investment banker agrees to sell securities only on a *best-efforts* basis, or as an agent for the company.
- The investment banker is not acting as an underwriter and receives a commission only on the sale of the stock.
- This arrangement may be advisable when the investment banker has doubts about the success of the securities offering.

Key 73 Public versus private placement of securities

OVERVIEW *Equity and debt securities may be issued publicly or privately. In a public issuance, securities are bought by the general public; in a private placement, the company issues securities directly to either one or a few large institutional investors. The institutional investors may be insurance companies, pension plans, commercial banks, etc.*

Consideration as to type to use:
- Nature and amount of financing
- Cost
- Marketability
- Exposure

Advantages of private placement versus public issuance:
- Quicker access to funds
- Lower costs for registering and selling the securities
- Avoidance of SEC filing requirements
- Avoidance of disclosure of information to the public at large
- Possibility for small companies to issue securities to the public when handling such a placement would not be profitable for an investment banker.

Disadvantages of private placement versus public issuance:
- There is greater difficulty in obtaining significant amounts of money
- Large institutional investors may scrutinize the company's activities more closely and have more stringent credit standards
- Large institutional investors are more capable of obtaining voting control of the company.

Key 74   Stockholders

OVERVIEW   *Stockholders are the owners of a corporation. There are preferred and common stockholders. A stock certificate is the evidence of ownership and indicates the shares, par value, and registered owner.*

Rights of common stockholders:
- Have voting rights
- Receive dividends
- Receive remaining net assets upon dissolution of the company.
- Entitled to preemptive right, allowing the stockholders to buy new shares before they are issued to the public in order to maintain proportionate percentage ownership.
- Have right to inspect the company's books.

Characteristics: Stockholders share in the company's financial success or failure since the market price of the stock and future dividend payments will be affected.
- Stockholders have limited liability and are not personally liable for the debts of the company.
- A company that publicly issues stock must abide by the regulatory requirements of the SEC and applicable stock exchange.

Key 75   Preferred stock

OVERVIEW   *Preferred stock is a hybrid security in that 1. it represents an equity investment in a firm, but 2. it has many of the features associated with a bond issue. Preferred stock is a class of capital stock that has preference over common stock in the event of corporate liquidation and in the distribution of earnings.*

Issuance: Preferred stock may be issued when the cost of common stock is high. The best time to issue preferred stock is when the company has excessive financial leverage and an issue of common stock might create control problems.

Characteristics: Preferred stock dividends are limited to the fixed rate specified, which is based on the total par value of the outstanding shares. See Key 58.
- In liquidation, preferred stockholders are paid after bondholders and before common stockholders. Preferred stockholders receive the par value of their shares, dividends in arrears, and the current year's dividend. The residual remaining goes to common stockholders.

Cumulative versus noncumulative preferred stock:
- *Cumulative preferred stock:* receives prior-year dividends, if they have not been paid, before common stockholders receive their dividends. Most preferred stock is cumulative.
- *Noncumulative preferred stock:* is not entitled to make up missed preferred dividends.

Participating versus nonparticipating preferred stock:
- *Participating preferred stock:* preferred and common stockholders participate in excess dividends if declared dividends exceed the amount normally given to preferred stockholders and common stockholders. Unless stated otherwise, the distribution of the excess dividends is based on the relative total par values. *Example:* If total par value of preferred stock and common stock are $50,000 and $150,000, respectively, *excess dividends* of $10,000 will be allocated as $2,500 to preferred and $7,500 to common stock in the ratio of 1/4 and 3/4.
- *Nonparticipating preferred stock:* preferred stock that does not participate in excess dividends. Most preferred stock is nonparticipating.

Advantages of issuing preferred stock: 1. preferred stockholders cannot force the company into bankruptcy, 2. preferred dividends do not have to be paid, whereas interest on debt must be paid, 3. preferred stock issuance does not dilute the ownership interest of common stockholders, 4. no collateral is required, whereas debt may require collateral, 5. preferred stockholders do not share in unusually high corporate earnings, and 6. a growth company may generate better earnings for its original owners by issuing preferred stock having a fixed dividend rate rather than by issuing common stock.

Disadvantages of issuing preferred stock: 1. preferred dividends are not tax deductible, and 2. preferred stock requires a higher yield than bonds because of the greater risk to the investor.

Advantages of investing in preferred stock: 1. preferred stockholders have priority over common stockholders if the company is declared bankrupt, and 2. preferred stock typically has a constant return in the form of a fixed dividend payment.

Disadvantages of investing in preferred stock: 1. if earnings are insufficient, the preferred dividend may be bypassed in the current year, 2. return is limited because of the fixed dividend rate, and 3. because of the absence of a maturity date, greater price variability exists with preferred stock than with bonds.

Key 76   Common stock

OVERVIEW   *Common stock are equity shares issued by the company to its stockholders.*

Common stock shares:
- *Authorized shares:* maximum amount of stock that may be issued according to the corporate charter.
- *Issued shares:* the number of authorized shares that have been sold to the public.
- *Treasury shares:* the number of previously issued shares that have been reacquired by the company.
- *Outstanding shares:* issued shares still held by the public. Outstanding shares equals issued shares less treasury shares.

Characteristics:
- Common stock is typically issued at a market price above par value. Par value is the stated amount per share on the stock certificates specified in the corporate charter.
- If debt is excessive, financing with equity is preferable.

Calculations:
- A determination of the number of shares that must be issued to raise sufficient funds to meet the capital budget may be required. This equals the funds needed divided by the market price per share.
- The estimated price per share at which to sell securities for a new company equals: $\dfrac{\text{Anticipated market value of the company}}{\text{Total shares outstanding}}$
- The expected rate of return on stock equals: $\dfrac{D_1}{P_o} + g$

  where

  D_1 = dividends per share in the current year

  P_o = market price per share

  g = growth rate in dividends (assumed constant)

Advantages of issuing common stock: 1. there is no repayment date; 2. company can omit dividend payment, 3. creates preemptive rights (see Key 77), and 4. improves debt/equity ratio.

Disadvantages of issuing common stock: 1. dividends are not tax-deductible, 2. ownership interest is diluted, 3. earnings and dividends are spread over more shares, 4. as more shares are issued, market price per share declines, and 5. the flotation costs of issuing common stock are higher than those for preferred stock or debt financing.

Key 77   Stock rights

OVERVIEW   *Stock rights represent the option to purchase securities at a specified price at a future date. The preemptive right provides existing stockholders with the first option to buy additional shares in the company. Exercising this right allows them to maintain voting control and protects against dilution in ownership and earnings.*

Ex rights or rights on: A rights offering has a date of record, which is the last day that the receiver of the right must be the legal owner in the company's stock ledger.
- *Ex rights:* stocks are sold without rights 4 business days before the record date.
- *Rights on:* stocks are sold with rights.

Characteristics of rights: The recipient of the rights can exercise them, sell them, or let them expire.
- The rights may be exercised for a given time period at a *subscription price,* established somewhat below the going market price.

Computations:
- After the subscription price has been determined, management computes the number of rights needed to buy one share of stock.

$$\text{Shares to be sold} = \frac{\text{Amount of funds to be obtained}}{\text{Subscription price}}$$

$$\text{Rights per share} = \frac{\text{Total shares outstanding}}{\text{Shares to be sold}}$$

- Theoretically, the value of a right should be the same whether the stock is selling with rights on or with ex rights.
- When stock is selling with rights on, the value of a right equals:

$$\frac{\text{Market value of stock with rights on} - \text{subscription price}}{\text{Number of rights needed to buy one share} + 1}$$

- When stock is traded ex rights, the market price is expected to drop by the value of the right. The market value of stock trading ex rights should equal:
Market value of stock with rights on less value of a right when stock is selling rights on
- The value of a right when stock is selling ex rights equals:

$$\frac{\text{Market value of stock trading ex rights} - \text{subscription price}}{\text{Number of rights needed to buy one new share}}$$

Key 78 Stock repurchases

OVERVIEW *Treasury stock is previously issued shares that have been reacquired by the company, resulting in a reduction in outstanding shares.*

Financial effect of repurchase: because there are fewer outstanding shares:
- fewer dividends will be paid
- earnings per share will increase (holding net income constant)
- market price per share will increase because of the increase in earnings per share.

Advantages of stock repurchase:
- Treasury stock may be used for future acquisitions or stock options
- If there is extra cash temporarily, may be a management strategy instead of paying a higher dividend that cannot be maintained
- If the price of the company's stock appreciates considerably, the stock can later be resold to the public at a significantly higher price.

Disadvantages of treasury stock acquisition:
- If investors believe that the company is engaging in a repurchase plan because management does not have alternative attractive investment options, market price of the stock may drop.
- If the reacquisition of stock appears to be intentional company manipulation of the price of the stock, problems with the SEC may arise.
- If the Internal Revenue Service (IRS) finds that the repurchase is designed to avoid the payment of tax on dividends, tax penalties may be imposed on the improper accumulation of earnings.

Key 79 Margin trading

OVERVIEW *Margin trading involves buying securities on credit, a form of leverage that magnifies the gains and losses from a given percentage of price fluctuation in securities.*

Initial margin requirement: minimum percentage of the purchase price that a margin customer must pay in cash. This requirement is currently at least 50 percent of the current market value of the security. Some securities may not be purchased on margin. The stockbroker lends the margin purchaser the money, retaining custody of the stock as collateral.
- A 60% margin requirement means that 100 shares of a stock selling for $200 a share can be purchased by putting up only 60% of the total purchase price in cash, that is, $12,000, borrowing the remaining $8,000.

Maintenance margin requirement: minimum percentage equity an investor must maintain in a stock or bond purchased using borrowed funds. The New York Stock Exchange and the National Association of Securities Dealers both require a maintenance margin in margin accounts equal to 25% of the market value of securities. Many brokerage firms require more, typically 30%.
- Investors who have securities worth less than the maintenance requirement are subject to a *margin call*.

Key 80 Short selling

OVERVIEW *Short selling means a security that is not owned by the seller. This method has been used to gain from a fall in stock price. In short selling, the investor wants to sell the stock high, hoping to buy it back later at a lower price. If the stock price falls, the investor makes money; if the stock price rises, the investor loses money.*

Short sale requirements: the seller must maintain a margin account with a stockbroker because the government and the brokerage house want to ensure that the investor will be able to buy back the stock if the price suddenly rises.
- The Federal Reserve requires that an investor have in the account cash or securities worth at least 50 percent of the market value of the stock being sold short.
- A listed stock can be sold short only when the stock price has risen. On the other hand, stocks traded over-the-counter may be sold short at any time.
- While the short-seller normally pays no interest charge, proceeds from the sale must be kept in the brokerage account.

Short sale strategies: since selling short can be extremely risky, the investor is advised to use short-selling only in certain cases:
- Go short because you think the stock price is going to decline
- Go short if you want to postpone making a gain and paying taxes on it from one year to the next
- Go short to protect yourself if you own the stock but for some reason cannot sell it. *Example:* If you buy stock through a payroll purchase plan at the end of each quarter but do not get the certificates until several weeks later, it may make sense to sell your shares short to lock in the gain.

Key 81   Governmental regulation

OVERVIEW *When securities issued to the public must conform to federal and state laws.*

Federal regulations:
- *Securities Act of 1933:* deals with regulation of new security issues. According to the Act: 1. it requires the *registration* of securities before they are sold to the public, 2. adequate disclosure of information must be made in a prospectus so potential investors may adequately appraise the issue, and 3. false representations and disclosures are prohibited.
- *Securities Exchange Act of 1934:* deals with regulation of existing security transactions. According to the Act: 1. registration of securities listed on the stock exchanges is required and manipulation is prohibited, 2. periodic disclosure of important financial information is mandatory, 3. holdings and transactions of officers and directors must be disclosed; 4. individuals owning 10% or more of equity securities must be identified along with their holdings, and 5. rules regarding proxy voting and margin requirements are spelled out.
- *Securities Act Amendments of 1975:* defines SEC authority and market determination of broker's commissions.

State regulations ("blue sky laws"): while state regulations may differ, they typically:
- protect investors from securities fraud
- require registration of new stock or debt issues
- require the disclosure of financial information about the securities issue.

Key 82   Efficient market theory

OVERVIEW   *An efficient market is one in which the market price of a stock is identical to its real (intrinsic) value. In an efficient market, all data are fully and immediately reflected in price. A price change may be positive or negative.*

Weak form of efficient market: No relationship exists between prior and future stock prices.
- Independence exists over time between prices.
- The value of historical information already lies in the current price. Therefore, reviewing past prices (technical analysis) is unimportant.

Semistrong form of efficient market: Stock price immediately reflects new information.
- Action after a known event produces random results.
- All public information is incorporated in a stock's value.
- Fundamental analysis (financial statement analysis) is not helpful in determining if a stock is over- or undervalued.

Strong form of efficient market: Stock prices reflect all information, public or private (insider).
- A perfect market exists.
- No individual or group has sole access to information.

Key 83 Convertible securities

OVERVIEW *A convertible security is one that may be exchanged for common stock by the holder according to agreed-upon terms. Examples are convertible bonds and convertible preferred stock. As the price of the underlying common stock increases, so will the price of the convertible security.*

Conversion statistics: The conversion ratio applies to the number of shares of stock the holder of the convertible security receives when the conversion is made.

$$\text{Conversion ratio} = \frac{\text{Face value of convertible security}}{\text{Conversion price}}$$

- The conversion price is the effective price the holder pays for the common stock when the conversion is effected. The conversion price is reduced by the percentage amount of any stock dividend or stock split so that the common stock shareholder maintains his or her proportionate interest.
- Conversion value of a security equals:

$$\text{Common stock price} \times \text{conversion ratio}$$

- When a convertible security is issued, it is priced higher than its conversion value.

$$\text{Conversion premium} = \frac{\text{Market value} - \text{conversion value}}{\text{Conversion value}}$$

- If the market price of common stock declines, a conversion does not occur, creating a *hung* security.

Valuation: A convertible security is a *hybrid* one, with characteristics similar to both bonds and common stock.
- Investment value is the value of the convertible security, assuming it was not convertible but had all its other attributes.
- The conversion value applies to the value of common stock received at the time the bond or preferred stock is converted.

Advantages of convertibles: 1. acts as a sweetener in a debt or preferred stock offering, 2. may pay a lower interest rate or preferred dividend yield, 3. is easier to market, 4. has less restrictive covenants, and 5. is a means of issuing common stock at a later date at a price higher than the current market price.

Disadvantages of convertibles: 1. the company will have to pay interest and principal on the convertible bond if the conversion is not made because the market price of the common stock fails to appreciate, and 2. if the market price of common stock does increase, the company would have been better off financing through a regular issue of common stock because it must now issue stock at a higher price.

Financing strategy:
- If the market price of common stock is depressed, convertible debt may be issued if market price of the common stock is expected to rise.
- The issuance of convertible debt may be advisable when the company wants to leverage itself in the short run but does not want to incur interest cost and pay principal in the long run.
- A convertible issue may be suggested for a growth company since the faster the growth rate, the earlier the conversion will take place.

Key 84   Stock warrants

OVERVIEW   *A stock warrant is the option to buy a specified number of shares of stock at a stated price. To obtain the common stock, the warrant must be given up, along with the payment of the* exercise price.

Detachable versus nondetachable warrants:
- *Detachable warrant:* is sold separately from the bond with which it is associated.
- *Nondetachable warrant:* is sold with its bond; both must be exercised simultaneously.

Characteristics:
- The issuing company typically receives funds for the warrants.
- A holder of a warrant may exercise it by buying the stock or selling the warrant to other investors or may continue to hold it.
- Warrants typically expire on a specified date; however, some warrants are perpetual.
- The exercise price of a warrant is usually fixed but is adjusted for stock dividends and stock splits.
- If the company's stock price goes up above the option price, the warrant will be exercised.

Valuation: The value of a warrant equals: market price per share − exercise price × number of shares that may be purchased through the exercise of the warrant
- The formula (theoretical) value is typically below the current market price of the warrant because the speculative appeal of a warrant allows the investor to obtain considerable leverage. The excess of the market price over its theoretical value is called a premium. The lowest amount that a warrant sells for is its theoretical value.
- The market value of a warrant depends on its convertibility into common stock.
- A warrant typically has a higher value if: 1. there is a relatively long active period remaining, 2. the dividend payment on the common stock is small, 3. the price of common stock is volatile, and 4. the common stock is listed on an exchange.

Advantages of warrants: 1. act as sweeteners for a debt or preferred stock issue, 2. allow bonds to be issued at a lower interest rate, and 3. allow for balanced financing between debt and equity.

Disadvantages of warrants: 1. dilute common stock when exercised, 2. there is high risk of losing the investment, 3. pay no dividends, and 4. have no voting rights.

Warrants versus convertible securities:

- The exercise of warrants generates funds for the company; exercise of convertibles does not.
- The exercise of warrants adds to stockholders' equity with total liabilities remaining the same. On the other hand, the conversion of a bond increases stockholders' equity and reduces total liabilities.

Theme 13 BUSINESS COMBINATIONS

*T*here are different types of business combinations: vertical, in which a company combines with a customer or supplier; horizontal, in which two companies in a similar business combines; and conglomerate, in which two companies in unrelated industries combine. A merger may result in many benefits, including reducing risk through diversification, improving overall financial condition, and obtaining a tax loss carryforward benefit. A holding company has as its major objective owning other companies. In some cases, an acquiring company may buy another business by going directly to the stockholders and buying their shares.

INDIVIDUAL KEYS IN THIS THEME	
85	Mergers and acquisitions
86	Holding company
87	Tender offer

Key 85   Mergers and acquisitions

OVERVIEW   *A merger is the combination of two or more companies into one; only the acquiring company retains its identity.*

Types of business combinations:
- *Vertical:* a company combines with a customer or supplier.
- *Horizontal:* two companies in a similar business combine.
- *Conglomerate:* two companies in unrelated industries combine.

Mergers:
- Buyers may use various financing packages for mergers, including common stock, preferred stock, convertible securities, cash, debt, and warrants.
- The acquiring company often issues stock according to a specified exchange ratio. A stock trade represents a tax-free exchange.
- When there is an exchange of cash for common stock, the selling firm's stockholders receive cash for their common stock, resulting in a taxable transaction.

Advantages of mergers: 1. diversification reduces risk, 2. there is a possible synergistic effect, 3. the company may obtain something it lacks, such as research capability, 4. a company may improve financial condition by combining with another financially strong company, 5. a good return on the investment may occur when the market value of the acquired company is materially below its replacement cost, and 6. acquiring company may obtain a tax loss carryforward benefit of the acquired company.

Disadvantages of mergers: 1. expected benefits (e.g., cost reductions) may not materialize, 2. friction may arise between the management of both companies, 3. antitrust action may block or delay the merger, and 4. dissenting minority stockholders may cause problems.

Considerations in determining acquisition terms: 1. the effect on dollar earnings and its growth rate which in turn impacts the P/E ratio, 2. dividends, 3. market price of the stock, 4. book value per share, 5. net working capital per share, and 6. liquidity.

Key 86 Holding company

OVERVIEW *A holding company has the sole purpose of owning the stock of other businesses. Acquiring a small percentage of another company (e.g., 20%) may be sufficient to obtain a significant influence over the other, particularly when stock ownership is widely dispersed.*

Characteristics:
- A company in a declining industry may want to move out of its basic operations by liquidating assets and using the funds obtained to invest in other companies with growth potential.
- Because the operating companies held by the holding company are distinct legal entities, the obligations of any one are isolated from the others.

Advantages of holding company:
- There is risk protection in that the failure of one company does not cause the failure of the other companies of the holding company.
- The holding company cannot lose more than its original investment.
- The holding company is able to acquire a large amount of assets with a small investment.
- It is possible to gain control of another business by buying sufficient shares in the market place.

Disadvantages of holding company:
- A holding company usually is more costly to administer than a single company resulting from a merger because economies of scale typically do not arise.
- There is multiple taxation because the subsidiary pays taxes on its earnings and the holding company pays taxes on the distributed dividends it receives.
- The U.S. Department of Justice may consider the holding company a near-monopoly and force dissolution of some of the companies by disposal of stock.
- A financial leverage effect may occur through increased debt necessitated by the acquisition of other companies. This will magnify either earnings or losses.

Key 87 Tender offer

OVERVIEW *A tender offer, usually in cash, is made by an acquiring company directly to stockholders of the company it wants to take over when the management of the target company does not want to be merged.*

Characteristics: Stockholders are induced to sell when the tender price significantly exceeds the current market price of the target common stock.
- Typically, there is an expiration date to the tender.
- Good takeover candidates are cash-rich businesses and those with low debt/equity ratios.

Disclosure requirements:
- The acquiring company must notify management of the targeted company and the Securities and Exchange Commission of its intentions 30 days before making its tender offer.
- The name of the group providing the money for the acquisition must be disclosed when significant amounts of stock are purchased on the stock exchange.
- Because of the disclosure rules, competitions may arise in the takeover attempt.

How to fight takeover attempts:
- Try to merge with a friendlier company.
- Initiate legal action to block takeover attempt.
- Furnish negative publicity about the raider.
- Purchase treasury stock to make fewer shares available for tendering.
- Give stockholders an attractive dividend to keep them happy.

Theme 14 FAILURE AND REORGANIZATION

A failing company may be able to arrange for a voluntary reduction in the amounts it owes creditors. However, creditors may insist upon a reorganization of the business if the company may get back on its feet. If things look hopeless, the company may be declared bankrupt and be liquidated. There are many signs of potential business failure, such as the Z score, that must be considered by creditors and investors.

INDIVIDUAL KEYS IN THIS THEME	
88	Voluntary settlement
89	Bankruptcy and reorganization

Key 88   Voluntary settlement

OVERVIEW   *A voluntary settlement with creditors allows the company to save many of the costs of a bankruptcy. Such a settlement is done out of court.*

Characteristics:
- The voluntary settlement enables the company to continue or be liquidated and is initiated to allow the debtor firm to recover some of its investment.
- A creditor committee may allow the business to continue in operation if it is anticipated that the company will recover.
- Creditors may also continue to do business with the company.

Extension: Creditors receive balances due over an extended time period. Current purchases are made with cash.
- Creditors may agree not only to lengthen the maturity date for payment but also to subordinate their claims to current debt for suppliers providing credit in the extension period.
- Creditors anticipate that the debtor will be able to work out the company's problems.
- The creditor committee may require certain controls over the company, such as approval for cash payments.
- If certain creditors object to the extension, they may be paid immediately so they cannot have the company declared bankrupt.

Composition: voluntary reduction of the amount the debtor owes the creditor. The creditor receives from the debtor a specified percentage of the obligation in full settlement of the debt.
- The debtor continues to operate.
- Court costs and the stigma of bankruptcy are eliminated.

Integration: a combined plan of extension, composition, and creditor control. *Example:* There may be a 10% cash down payment and five 10% future payments in the form of notes, for a total payment of 60%. The remaining 40% is forgiven.

Advantages of negotiated settlement: 1. creditors usually wind up with more than in bankruptcy, 2. settlement is less costly because it avoids or reduces legal fees, and 3. settlement is less formal and easier to implement than bankruptcy proceedings.

Disadvantages of negotiated settlement: 1. if the debtor continues in the business, there may be a further decline in asset values, and 2. unrealistic small creditors may drain the negotiating process.

Key 89 Bankruptcy and reorganization

OVERVIEW *When a company fails, it can either be reorganized or be dissolved depending upon the circumstances. In bankruptcy, liabilities exceed the fair market value of assets and there exists a negative real net worth. A company may also fail because of technical insolvency—an inability to satisfy current debt when due even though total assets exceed total liabilities.*

Possible reasons for business failure: 1. poor financial and operating management, 2. economic downturn, 3. end of company life cycle, 4. loss of lawsuit, 5. overexpansion, and 6. catastrophe.

Bankruptcy and reorganization:
- If no voluntary settlement is agreed to for a financially distressed company, it may be put into bankruptcy by its creditors.
- A company may file for reorganization under which it will formulate a plan for continued life.
- Chapter 7 of the Bankruptcy Reform Act of 1978 outlines the procedures to be followed for liquidation.
- Chapter 11 describes the steps of reorganizing a failed business.
- If reorganization is not possible under Chapter 11, the company will be liquidated in accordance with Chapter 7.
- Types of reorganization are *voluntary,* in which the company petitions for its own reorganization, and *involuntary,* in which creditors file for an involuntary reorganization of the company.

Steps in reorganization:
1. A reorganization petition is filed under Chapter 11.
2. A judge approves the petition and either appoints a trustee or allows the creditors to elect one to handle the disposition of the assets.
3. The trustee presents a reorganization plan to the court.
4. The plan is given to the creditors and stockholders for approval.
5. The debtor pays professional service fees in connection with the reorganization.

Liquidation due to bankruptcy: A firm that cannot be effectively reorganized is liquidated.

- In many cases, the proceeds from liquidation will be insufficient to pay off stockholders.
- After claims have been paid, a discharge in bankruptcy occurs in which the court releases the company from legitimate debts in bankruptcy. However, there may be certain debts immune to discharge.
- If a debtor has not been discharged within the previous 6 years or was not bankrupt because of fraud, the debtor may then start a new business.

Claim priority: The following rank order exists in meeting claims:

1. *Secured claims:* If the value of the secured assets is insufficient, the balance reverts to general creditor status.
2. *Bankruptcy administrative costs:* These include trustee, legal, and accounting.
3. *Unsecured salaries and commissions:* up to a limit per individual within the prescribed time period.
4. *Unsecured customer deposits:* up to a limit.
5. *Taxes due.*
6. *General creditor claims:* claims by creditors who do not have collateral supporting the amounts due. *Examples:* accounts payable and debentures.
7. *Preferred stockholders.*
8. *Common stockholders.*

Glossary

accounts receivable turnover
Annual credit sales divided by average accounts receivable.

acid-test ratio
The most liquid current assets (cash, marketable securities, and accounts receivable) divided by current liabilities.

additional paid-in capital
Excess received from stockholders over par value of the stock issued.

annual report
Evaluation prepared by companies at the end of the reporting year.

annuity
Series of equal periodic payments or receipts.

asset turnover
Sales divided by average total assets, revealing the efficiency of corporate assets in generating revenue.

banker's acceptance
Time draft drawn by a business firm whose payment is guaranteed by the bank's "acceptance" of it.

bankruptcy
Situation in which a firm's liabilities exceed the fair value of its assets.

beta
The variability in the price of a stock relative to the variability in a stock market index.

bond
Written promise by a company to pay the face amount at the maturity date.

book value per share
Worth of each share of stock per the books based on historical cost.

break-even point
The level of sales where total costs equal total revenue.

bridge loan

Short-term loan that is made in expectation of intermediate- or long-term loans.

budget

Quantitative plan of activities and programs expressed in terms of assets, liabilities, revenues, and expenses.

business cycle

Recurrence of periods of contracting and expanding economic conditions.

callable bond

Bond issue with a call (buy back) provision.

capital asset pricing model (CAPM)

Theory of asset pricing used to analyze the relationship between risk and rates of return in securities.

capital budgeting

Process of making long-term planning decisions for capital investments.

capital rationing

Selecting the mix of acceptable projects that provides the highest overall *net present value* of future cash flows when a company has a limit on the budget for capital spending.

capital structure

Composition of common stock, preferred stock, retained earnings, and long-term debt maintained by the business entity in financing its assets.

cash flow

Cash receipts minus cash disbursements.

common stock

Share evidencing equity ownership in a company.

convertible security

Type of stock or bond that can be voluntarily converted into capital stock at a later date.

cost of capital Weighted average of the costs of debt and equity funds.

coupon rate Interest rate on the face amount of a debt security.

credit line Specified amount of money available to a borrower from a bank, usually for one year.

current ratio Current assets divided by current liabilities.

debenture Long-term debt instrument that is not secured by a mortgage or other lien on specific property.

debt-equity ratio Total liabilities divided by total stockholders' equity.

economic order quantity Size that minimizes the sum of carrying and ordering costs.

effective interest rate Real rate of interest on a loan equal to the nominal interest divided by the proceeds of the loan.

face value Nominal amount of a debt obligation or equity security as stated in the instrument.

factoring Outright sale of a firm's accounts receivable to another party (the factor) *without recourse*, which means the factor must bear the risk of collection.

financial leverage Portion of a firm's assets financed with debt instead of equity.

financial statement Report containing financial information about a company.

holding company	Corporation owning enough voting stock in another company to control its policies and management.
indenture	Legal document that specifically states the conditions under which a bond has been issued, the rights of the bondholders, and the duties of the issuing corporation.
insolvency	Failure of a company to meet its obligations as they become due.
inventory turnover	Cost of goods sold divided by average inventory.
investment banker	Intermediary between an issuer of new securities and the investor.
lease	Legal agreement whereby the lessee uses real or personal property of the lessor for a rental charge.
leveraged buyout	Acquisition of one company by another, typically with borrowed funds.
liquidity	Ability of current assets to meet current liabilities when due.
lockbox	Box in a United States Postal Service facility, used to facilitate collection of customer remissions.
maturity value	Amount to be paid on the maturity date of a financial instrument.
nominal interest rate	Stated interest rate on the face of a debt security or loan.
opportunity cost	Revenue forfeited by rejecting an alternative use of time or facilities.

payback period	Length of time required to recover the initial amount of a capital investment.
preferred stock	Class of capital stock that has preference over common stock in the event of corporate liquidation and in the distribution of earnings.
present value	Current worth of future sums of money.
prime interest rate	Interest rate charged by banks to their most financially sound customers.
prospectus	Document that must accompany a new issue of securities.
reorder point	Inventory level at which it is appropriate to replenish stock.
safety stock	Extra units of inventory carried as protection against possible stockouts.
stock option	Right given the holder to buy a specified number of shares of stock at a certain price by a particular date.
stock right	Privilege giving current stockholders the first right to buy shares in a new offering, thus maintaining their proportionate ownership interest.
stock split	Issuance of substantial amount of additional shares, thus reducing the par value of the stock on a proportionate basis.
tender offer	Bid to buy stock of a company at a specified price (usually at a premium over the market price) to gain control of the company.

INDEX